CULTURES OF THE WORLD
Finland

Cavendish
Square

New York

Published in 2017 by Cavendish Square Publishing, LLC
243 5th Avenue, Suite 136, New York, NY 10016
Copyright © 2017 by Cavendish Square Publishing, LLC

Third Edition

CPSIA Compliance Information: Batch #CW17CSQ

All websites were available and accurate when this book was sent to press.

Library of Congress Cataloging-in-Publication Data

Names: Tan, Chung Lee, 1949- author. | Schmermund, Elizabeth, co-author.
Title: Finland / Tan Chung Lee and Elizabeth Schmermund.
Description: New York : Cavendish Square Publishing, [2017] | Series: Cultures of the world | Includes bibliographical references and index.
Identifiers: LCCN 2016041208 (print) | LCCN 2016042116 (ebook) | ISBN 9781502622273 (library bound) | ISBN 9781502622280 (E-book)
Subjects: LCSH: Finland--Juvenile literature.
Classification: LCC DL1012 .T35 2017 (print) | LCC DL1012 (ebook) | DDC 948.97--dc23
LC record available at https://lccn.loc.gov/2016041208

Writers, Chung Lee Tan; Elizabeth Schmermund (third edition)
Editorial Director, third edition: David McNamara
Editor, third edition: Debbie Nevins
Associate Art Director, third edition: Amy Greenan
Designer, third edition: Jessica Nevins
Production Coordinator, third edition: Karol Szymczuk
Cover Picture Researcher: Angela Siegel
Picture Researcher, third edition: Jessica Nevins

PICTURE CREDITS

Dave Bartruff/Getty Images, cover; Sonia Alves-Polidori/Shutterstock.com, 1; snowturtle/Shutterstock.com, 3; Kekyalyaynen/Shutterstock.com, 5; Vladimir Nenezic/Shutterstock.com, 6; Globe Turner/Shutterstock.com, 8; Magdanatka/Shutterstock.com, 12; Sandra Kemppainen/Shutterstock.com, 13; Scanrail1/Shutterstock.com, 14; Jarmo_Honkala/iStock/Thinkstock, 17; Vitaly Titov/Shutterstock.com, 18; Dcoetzee/File:Attributed to Jacob Hoefnagel Gustavus Adolphus, King of Sweden 16111632 Google Art Project.jpg/Wikimedia Commons, 21; Anders E. Skanberg/Shutterstock.com, 23; vsdn.ru/File:Alexander I of Russia by G.Dawe (1826, Peterhof).jpg/Wikimedia Commons, 24; Stormfront/File:Skiis and guns.jpg/Wikimedia Commons, 26; posztos/Shutterstock.com, 30; Michał Józefaciuk/File:Sauli Niinistö Senate of Poland 2015.JPG/Wikimedia Commons, 33; Meißner/ullstein bild via Getty Images, 35; Popova Valeriya/Shutterstock.com, 37; Aija Lehtonen/Shutterstock.com, 38; meunierd/Shutterstock.com, 41; peshyuri/Shutterstock.com, 42; Taina Sohlman/Shutterstock.com, 45; Ivannn/Shutterstock.com, 46; Roman Vukolov/Shutterstock.com, 48; Markus Mainka/Shutterstock.com, 49; ANTTI AIMO-KOIVISTO/AFP/Getty Images, 51; Sinelev/Shutterstock.com, 52; Popova Valeriya/Shutterstock.com, 55; PlusONE/Shutterstock.com, 56; TristanBM/Shutterstock.com, 60; Nasjonalbiblioteket of Norway/File:Lapper og Reinsdyr.jpg/Wikimedia Commons, 62; Alison Wright/National Geographic/Getty Images, 65; elina/Shutterstock.com, 67; Eugene Sergeev/Shutterstock.com, 68; Nadia Virronen/Shutterstock.com, 70; Tanhu/Shutterstock.com, 71; Mika Heittola/Shutterstock.com, 72; Markku Heikkilä/Moment/Getty Images, 74; Kristiina Kontoniemi/Folio/Getty Images, 75; Kaisa Q/Moment/Getty Images, 78; futureGalore/Shutterstock.com, 80; SergeyP/Shutterstock.com, 82; Cecil File:Mikael Agricola, Pernå.jpg/Wikimedia Commons, 83; www.nationalmuseum.se/File:John III of Sweden.jpg/Wikimedia Commons, 84; Grisha Bruev/Shutterstock.com, 85; Veikko Wahlroos/AFP/Getty Images, 86; Ms Jane Campbell/Shutterstock.com, 88; Bo Zaunders/Corbis Documentary/Getty Images, 93; Danita Delimont/Gallo Images/Getty Images, 94; Kaihsu Tai/File:Metallimessu.jpg/Wikimedia Commons, 98; David Levy/File:Jean Sibelius, 1913.jpg/Wikimedia Commons, 100; Nadezda Slobodinskaya/Shutterstock.com, 103; Prolog/File:Paavo Nurmi and Wäinö Aaltonen.jpg/Wikimedia Commons, 104; Max Topchii/Shutterstock.com, 106; Tanhu/Shutterstock.com, 109; Pitke/File:Vippi.jpg/Wikimedia Commons, 111; Grisha Bruev/Shutterstock.com, 112; JOHN MACDOUGALL/AFP/Getty Images, 113; BlueOrange Studio/Shutterstock.com, 116; Markus Rantala/File:Unikeonpäivä, Naantali, 27.7.2012 (25).JPG/Wikimedia Commons, 119; Kati Molin/Shutterstock.com, 124; kaband/Shutterstock.com, 127; Lilyana Vynogradova/Shutterstock.com, 128; extremechan/Shutterstock.com, 130; pingpongcat/Shutterstock.com, 131; Globe Turner/Shutterstock.com, 137.

PRECEDING PAGE

Finns enjoy a sunny afternoon on Suommenlinna Island.

Printed in the United States of America

CONTENTS

FINLAND TODAY

TO PEOPLE WHO ARE UNFAMILIAR WITH ALL THAT FINLAND HAS TO OFFER, they may only know the country due to its northern location and frigid winters, or perhaps for its well-regarded social systems. While it's true that Finland's temperatures can dip into the uncomfortably cold range, the country also boasts one of the largest amounts of lakes, among the lushest forests, and the most sparsely populated land per capita of any country in Europe. Although today most Finns live in urban areas, they also have ample opportunities to enjoy the natural beauty of their homeland. The natural world has become integrated into Finnish culture itself, with cuisine built on fresh and seasonally available ingredients, a tradition of outdoor sports on every level of play, from the pros to family outings, and prevalent hobbies like berry picking and mushroom foraging.

When mentioning national favorite pastimes of the Finns, it would be remiss not to mention the sauna. When the temperatures dip too low, Finns head into their saunas to relax physically and mentally, or to socialize with friends. Oftentimes, a trip to the sauna is followed by a quick jump into the snow to cool off and rejuvenate one's senses. Indeed, saunas are integral to Finnish culture and linked with the Finns'

Saunas are an integral part of Finnish culture.

love of nature. The Finnish sauna has ancient roots and dates back to at least the sixteenth century. In fact, hundreds of years ago, the Finnish sauna was even more versatile than it is today. It served as not only a bath, but could also be lived in and could house a rudimentary kitchen. Before the birth of modern hospitals, Finnish women even gave birth in saunas! Today, saunas are omnipresent in Finland. They sit in heavily wooded forests, are tucked adjacent to lake houses, or are even outfitted into Finns' apartment buildings. The deepest sauna in the world was built 4,600 feet (1,400 meters) down in the Pyhäsalmi Mine in central Finland, which is also the second deepest metal mine in Europe. One sauna is even housed within the Finnish parliament. Saunas are traditionally used on Saturdays but can be enjoyed any day of the week. The Finns love to jump into their saunas in summer as much as in winter, and three million saunas—an average of one per household—are used by five million Finns!

But it isn't just nature and traditional culture that have shaped Finland and its people. Finland has a complex history and was politically dominated for centuries by Sweden and then Russia. These cultures have left their own imprint on Finnish life. They have also imbued the Finns with a spirit of adaptability, quiet strength, and survivability. There is even a Finnish word for this national character: *sisu*. Described by the *New York Times* as the Finns' "favorite word" and "the most wonderful of all their words," sisu, which is not easily translatable into English, means all of the following: persistence, determination, courage, adaptability, and rationality in the face of adversity. According to Finlandia University, "Sisu is the quality that lets [Finns] pick up, move on, and learn something from previous failures. It's the hard-jawed integrity that makes them pay their war debts in full. In short, it's the indomitable will that sets Finns apart and explains many of the incredible things they do."

And the Finns have accomplished many incredible things. They have revolutionized modern design and art nouveau architecture. Their music, from the famous composer Jean Sibelius to singer Olavi Virta to contemporary rock band HIM, has been played on airwaves globally and inspired generations. But perhaps the most visible signs of their success are in entrepreneurship and the economy. Over the past several decades, Finland has revolutionized high-tech fields. Finnish companies like Nokia, one of the world's most popular cell-phone companies, pioneered the first cell phones. Finns are well educated in math and science, and they are inculcated into a field of high technology and development. They also enjoy one of the highest global literacy rates and read more than almost any other national group in the world.

Perhaps another reason for Finland's success has been its focus on taking care of its people. Finland is known, like the other Nordic countries, for its "social safety net," or its programs that contribute to a high quality of life for its people. Finns today enjoy low-cost and public health insurance, pioneering programs in family and parental leave, and fewer hours per week in high-stress jobs. This doesn't mean that Finns don't like to work; but it does mean that they value their relationships with their friends and family, as well as with the natural world. This has resulted in a strong community upon which Finns can rely in times of need. According to the Organisation for Economic Co-operation and Development's Better Life Index, 94 percent of Finns know they could rely on someone during challenging times. (Compare this to the average of 88 percent among nations.)

And the Finns have indeed lived through challenging times. Finland, like many other European countries, was adversely affected by the global economic crisis that began in the United States in 2008. As of 2016, Finland is still struggling to return to its high point of economic activity. This struggle is intensified by the aging of Finland's population, which has negative effects for the country's labor force. According to the *Economist*, the number of Finns aged sixteen to sixty-four is shrinking by nearly 0.5 percent per year. But this doesn't mean that tough economic times are all that's in store for Finland. The country continues to lead globally in innovation and entrepreneurship, an outgrowth of sisu that is historically Finnish. Of all countries, Finland—and its people—has found new ways to innovate and survive, no matter what tests the nation may face in the coming years.

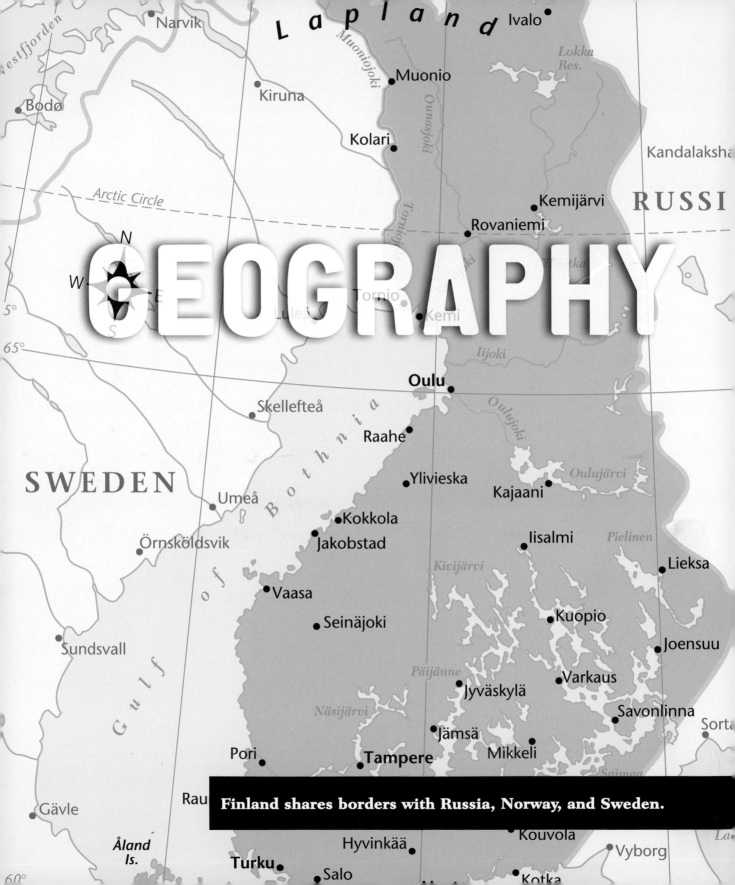

GEOGRAPHY

Finland shares borders with Russia, Norway, and Sweden.

FINLAND IS PART OF THE NORDIC countries, a region in northwestern Europe that also includes Denmark, Iceland, Norway, and Sweden. But Finland is also unique among these countries. It is the northernmost country in Europe, and one-quarter of its land area extends beyond the Arctic Circle. Finland also lies on the edge of continental Europe, sharing its eastern border with Russia. With a total land area of 130,558 square miles (338,144 square kilometers), it is one of the largest countries in Europe—although it holds a population of only 5.5 million people, which is approximately the population of the city of Miami.

The country is surrounded by land except for a 680-mile-long (1,100-kilometer-long) stretch of coastline to the south and west along the gulfs of Finland and Bothnia. From north to south, the country extends 720 miles (1,160 km). From east to west, it stretches 335 miles (540 km). Finland shares a border to the north with Norway, to the west with Sweden, and to the east with Russia.

Finland is largely forested, with over 70 percent of its land covered in dense evergreen and oak forests. Only 8 percent of the country is made up of cultivated land, while 13 percent is made up of swamps, alpine tundra, sandy coasts, and other landforms.

THE LANDSCAPE

Finland's landscape was sculpted by both fire and ice. About forty million years ago, ancient volcanic islands began colliding and forming the bedrock beneath the country, which is among the world's oldest. At the end of the last ice age, approximately ten thousand years ago, gigantic glaciers slowly receded back to the Arctic, scratching the bedrock and carving out the features that we see today. Evidence of this glacial shift is apparent in the lake basins, which still bear the scrape marks from the glaciers' movement, as well as the geological debris deposited at Salpausselkä Ridge. Ridges, called eskers, formed from the powerful currents of the melting glaciers around these lake basins.

Since the disappearance of the continental glaciers, the country's land mass has been rising from the sea in a process known as isostatic uplift. As the continental glaciers shift, they have the effect of depressing the land over which they travel; but when the weight of the ice is lifted after the glaciers move on, the land rises. Even though it has been ten thousand years since the last ice sheets receded, Finland is still recovering from this immense load. The land along the Gulf of Finland, for example, rises 12 inches (30 centimeters) every one hundred years, while on the Gulf of Bothnia, it goes up by as much as 36 inches (90 cm) during the same period of time. It is estimated that Finland's total land mass increases by 2.7 square miles (7 sq km) each year. Most of the land along the coast comprises low-lying plains. Inland, there are mounds and hills interspersed with lakes and rivers.

Finland is such a long country that the landscape from south to north varies greatly; the gently rolling rural landscape in the south gradually gives way to hills and vast forested areas in the north. The only mountainous area in the country is in the northwest, near Norway, in an area known as Upland Finland, where peaks average 3,300 feet (1,000 m). The exception is Haltiatunturi, which at 4,343 feet (1,324 m) is Finland's highest point.

More than two-thirds of Finland is covered with forest. Finland has more forest area per capita than any other country in Europe with approximately 9.8 acres (4 hectares) of forest per person. Wild animals such as elk, bears, and, occasionally, wolves roam the forests of spruce, birch, and pine. In the foothills of Lapland—a region above the Arctic Circle comprising not only a part of Finland but also parts of Sweden, Norway, and Russia—herds of reindeer wander freely.

FINLAND PROPER

Southwest Finland, located along the coast, is also known as Finland Proper. This is because, hundreds of years ago, the area was populated by the ethnic Finns, called *suomalaiset* in Finnish. This area is popular with tourists, who visit its main centers—Helsinki, the capital, and Turku, the former capital— in droves to enjoy manor houses and medieval castles. In the west, the Gulf of Bothnia forms a natural border between Finland and its neighbor, Sweden. To the south, the Gulf of Finland, which along with the Gulf of Bothnia forms two arms of the Baltic Sea, separates the country from Estonia, Latvia, and the coast of Russia.

A look at a map of Finland shows an archipelago of seventeen thousand tree-covered islands and smaller skerries (small, rocky islands, or reefs) scattered off its coast, extending right up to the Åland Islands. The waters around this scenic archipelago are a yachtsman's paradise.

THE LAND OF LAKES

The Finnish Lake District is one of the country's geographical treasures, where 188,000 lakes were gouged out by receding glaciers thousands of years ago. This district comprises most of the central and eastern regions of Finland and is bordered in the south by the Salpausselkä Ridges. The largest lake in Finland is Lake Saimaa, which stretches 443 square miles (200 sq km) and forms part of the Saimaa lake system, which extends 1,850 square miles (4,790 sq km). The Lake District stretches into Russia, as there is no natural border between the two countries.

The beautiful lakelands are at the heart of Finland, occupying almost one-third of the whole country. Thousands of lakes flow down the many rivers to drain into the Baltic Sea. Before the days of roads and railways, the lakes formed narrow waterways that linked towns across central Finland. Ships were the only means of travel. Today, one can travel through central Finland by road, in addition to the more traditional route on board a passenger ship.

LAPLAND AND THE ARCTIC CIRCLE

The largest region of Finland is located in and above the Arctic Circle. Called Lapland, it is also the country's most sparsely populated area. Here, the beauty of the natural environment shines. Lapland is known as the land of the midnight sun. Because of its northern location, the region experiences seventy days of constant sunlight followed by a fifty-day "sunset" as the sun lowers in the horizon. Then, for six months, the sun rests below the horizon. But even in darkness the region hosts its natural splendors: this is the season of the aurora borealis, also known as the northern lights, when splashes of brilliant colors dance across the dark sky.

The northern lights dance across the sky above Lapland.

Visitors to Finland are assured of seeing the midnight sun between May 17 and June 25. At the peak of summer in northern Finland, the sun is above the horizon twenty-four hours a day. In Utsjoki, the northernmost municipality of Finland and the European Union, the longest summer day occurs over a two-month period. Even in southern Finland, there is no complete darkness during the night—the long evening twilight merges with an equally long morning dawn.

Many people visit Lapland to experience the midnight sun, or *kaamos*. In addition, Lapland's great wilderness is a big attraction. Lapland, which occupies one-third of the land area of Finland, has plenty of open space and herds of roaming reindeer. Unlike the rest of Finland, there are few lakes in Lapland, but there are many rivers separated by vast stretches of uninhabited land. Lots of pine and spruce can be found in the valleys. Above the valleys are fells, which are gently rounded hills that are the result of the erosion by glaciers. The fells are treeless except for occasional scrub.

FINLAND'S CAPITAL

Helsinki is Finland's newest capital. Although it was inaugurated in 1812, the city boasts hundreds of years of cultural history. Located in the region of Uusimaa, on the coast of the Gulf of Finland, it is the northernmost capital of any European country. Helsinki is a unique intersection of the cultures that have marked the region, including Estonian, Swedish, and Russian heritages. In recent years, it has often made the top of the world's most livable cities list due to its cultural attractions, educational institutions, safety, and proximity to nature.

Helsinki, Finland's capital, boasts colorful buildings and a busy harbor.

Founded in 1550, Helsinki was known in Swedish as Helsingfors. In 1748, the Swedes built a castle on the island of Suomenlinna, just outside the city. Yet there is also much about Helsinki that reminds visitors of the period when Finland was governed by Russia as a grand duchy. In particular, there is the magnificent Senate Square, with its Lutheran cathedral and surrounding neoclassical buildings, designed by Carl Ludwig Engel from 1818 to 1822 to commemorate Finland's integration into the Russian Empire. The Uspenski Orthodox Cathedral, with its gilded onion domes, and the city's many Russian restaurants add to Helsinki's czarist flavor. Architecturally, Helsinki bears such a great resemblance to czarist Saint Petersburg that several US movies with Russian settings have been shot on location in Helsinki instead of in Russia.

The city is also known for its art nouveau buildings that were built in the 1900s. The best example of art nouveau is visible in the work of Eliel Saarinen and his striking design of the Helsinki Central Railway Station. The presence of many parks and Helsinki's location on the coastline of the Baltic Sea make for an attractive and scenic setting. With a population of only 630,000, the city is not congested and has many open spaces.

FINLAND'S LARGEST URBAN AREA

Outside of Helsinki, Tampere is the largest urban area in Finland, as well as the most populous inland city of any Nordic country. With a population of about 223,000 and growing, Tampere was once a manufacturing center, similar to Manchester in England. This gave the city its nickname of "Manse." Located between the lakes of Näsijärvi and Pyhäjärvi in southwest Finland, this beautiful setting was also convenient for industries. Today, Tampere is best known for its culture. Many of Finland's most famous writers were born or lived in the city, and the popular music scene there has led to a genre of Finnish rock, called "Manserock," being named after it. Music is an important part of Tampere's cultural identity. It hosts Tammerfest, a youth rock festival, every July, and three international music events are held in the city every year.

FINLAND'S OLDEST CITY

Turku was once Finland's capital. It is the country's oldest city and remains its main port to this day. With a population of approximately 180,000 inhabitants, the city is the sixth largest in Finland. The word *turku* comes from the East Slavic word for "marketplace," alluding to the historical commercial importance of the city. Founded in the thirteenth century, it became a thriving center of trade and served as the capital of Finland until 1812. Today, many tourists visit Turku to take in its historical sites, including the famous medieval Turku Castle. First built in 1280, the castle once served as Finland's main defense during several important battles. Today it is Finland's most-visited museum

Another medieval attraction, Turku Cathedral, took two centuries to complete after construction started in the thirteenth century. Many well-known figures in Finnish history are buried in the main cathedral and its side chapels. The scenic beauty of Turku can best be appreciated by taking a cruise and sailing among its many islands.

A SURPRISINGLY TEMPERATE CLIMATE

Finland's climate is moderated by the Baltic Sea, inland waters, and airflows from the Atlantic Ocean (warmed by an extension of the Gulf Stream), making it warmer than other locations at similarly northern latitudes, like Greenland and Siberia. Changes in temperature are often caused by shifting winds, with westerly breezes bringing warm and clear weather. While the country enjoys an annual average temperature of 62 degrees Fahrenheit (17 degrees Celsius), sometimes southern and southeastern winds from the Asian continent extend into Finland, causing extreme heat waves in the summer or abnormally cold spells in the winter.

There are regional differences in the climate as well as variations in the seasons. Winter is a long season in the north, with snow arriving as early as October and lasting until late April in Lapland. In the south, the first snow appears in December and days are short, lasting under six hours. The average winter temperature in the south is 26°F (-3°C).

Summers in Finland are warm. In the south, the temperature in July averages 68°F (20°C), although it can climb to 86°F (30°C) during the day. The south also receives 8 inches (20 cm) more rain than in the north; on the average, the country has about one hundred days of rain each year.

PLANTS AND ANIMALS

Although Finland is located at an extreme northern latitude, it is more temperate than other locations at the same latitude because it is located on the Gulf Stream. Nearly three-quarters of the country is covered by forests and, indeed, most of Finland lies in the northern coniferous forest zone. Because of its location, Finland has a shorter growing season and a limited amount of tree species. There are four coniferous tree species native to Finland, including Scots pine, Norway spruce, and silver and downy birch. Oak trees can also be found in the extreme south of the country.

There are at least sixty different species of mammals native to Finland. Common animals include the wolf, European brown bear, lynx, wolverine, and Saimaa seals, while reindeer, beavers, and Finnish deer are also abundant. Some animals, such as moose, are so numerous that hunting is permitted to control their populations. Foxes, squirrels, and hare are plentiful in the forests.

There are more than 350 bird species in Finland, and most of them are migratory. Native bird species include the blackbird, white-tailed eagle, osprey, eagle, and whooping swan, which is Finland's national bird. The white-tailed eagle was once considered an endangered species, but it is now increasing in number.

Fish are plentiful, and more than seventy species can be found in Finland. The commercially important ones are the Baltic herring and whitefish. Reptiles and frogs are less common, with eleven species found in the country. The most common snake is the European adder or common viper.

FINLAND'S PINNIPEDS

Pinnipeds are better known by their common English name: seals. In Finland, many species of seals dot the icy waters of the coast. Four seal species are native to the country and can be found there year-round.

But the lake seal, and the Saimaa ringed seal in particular, are the rarest pinnipeds in Finland. These inland seals were forced to adapt to freshwater lakes thousands of years ago, when the lakes were cut off from the ocean. Found in Lake Saimaa, Finland's largest lake, the Saimma ringed seal is among the most endangered seal species in the world. They number only 320 and are found only in Lake Saimma. Finland works hard to protect these special seals and proudly featured the Saimma ringed seal on its five markka coin before it adopted the euro as its currency in 2002.

INTERNET LINKS

www.worldatlas.com/webimage/countrys/europe/fi.htm
Explore maps of Finland and find information about the country's history here.

www.worldtravelguide.net/finland/weather-climate-geography
Information about Finland's geography and climate can be found at this World Travel Guide site.

HISTORY

The fifteenth-century Olavinlinna Castle is located in Savonlinna, Finland.

TRADITIONALLY, IT WAS THOUGHT that Finland was first settled following the last ice age, in approximately 9000 BCE. However, contemporary archaeological discoveries have questioned this accepted history. Recent excavations of Wolf Cave, located in Kristinestad, in the Pyhävuori Mountains, suggest that the area was inhabited by Neanderthals some 120,000 to 130,000 years ago. If this is confirmed, this would be the first proof of Neanderthals having lived in any Nordic country.

The ancestors of today's Finnish people are believed to have migrated to Finland from hunter-gatherer communities in modern-day Estonia, Latvia, Poland, and Russia. There is evidence that the area of Finland above the Arctic Circle was occupied during the Stone Age, from approximately 7500 to 1500 BCE. During the Bronze Age (1500—500 BCE) and Iron Age (500 BCE—400 CE), these first settlers moved from the coastal areas inland, trading and developing cultural ties with other groups of people to the east and west. The restless Vikings, during the eighth to eleventh centuries, developed ties with neighboring peoples in other Nordic countries and Russia. Vikings raided and traded as far west as the contemporary United States and as far east as present-day

Many runes the cold has told me, / Many lays the rain has brought me, / Other songs the winds have sung me. / Many birds from many forests, / Oft have sung me lays n concord / Waves of sea, and ocean billows, / Music from the many waters, / Music from the whole creation, / Oft have been my guide and master.
—From the *Kalevala*

Istanbul. Some believe that the Finns participated in these Viking campaigns. Vikings also settled both on the islands of Finland and its mainland. Eventually, western Scandinavians were converted to Christianity in the early- to mid-twelfth century, which ended their pirating campaigns. The Finns continued to travel and trade across vast swaths of water and land, and their folktales, passed down orally for generations, about these adventures were compiled in the epic *Kalevala*, published in the nineteenth century.

SWEDISH CONTROL

Until the mid-thirteenth century, different tribes who controlled different swaths of land populated Finland. With no central authority, neighboring countries, including Sweden and Denmark, clamored to gain control over the land. During this period of time, the three main tribes occupying Finland also entered into various conflicts with one another. The Finns were located in the southwest of Finland, called Finland Proper, while the Tavastians lived inland in southern Finland, and the Karelians inhabited the east.

Sweden, at that time under the influence of the Roman Catholic Church and the Russian city of Novgorod, sought to gain political control over this fractious country. It began its encroachment upon Finland in the twelfth century. The first crusade in 1155, led by King Eric and Saint Henry, the bishop of Uppsala, was launched to increase Swedish influence. Missionaries conducted their work around Turku and the inner areas around Tampere. Christianity was firmly established in southwest Finland in the mid-twelfth century. After the pope gave his sanction in 1216, the Swedes continued their quest with a second crusade into Tavastia. They entered Häme, Uusimaa, and Karelia, where they built a castle. Soon, Swedish immigrants moved in to settle along the coast. In the meantime, Novgorod was trying to extend its influence along the Gulf of Finland and the area around Lake Ladoga, while Denmark and Germany were gaining control of the coastal regions along the eastern route.

In 1293, Sweden and Novgorod continued their battle for the control of Finland and the eastern coast of the Gulf of Finland when Sweden built the mighty Wiborg fortress and city. In 1300, Sweden established a fort on the banks of the River Neva that was later destroyed by Novgorod.

The war finally ended in 1323 with the Treaty of Pähkinäsaari, which established a border between Sweden and Novgorod for the first time. The eastern part of Karelia was made part of Novgorod, linking it to Russia and the Orthodox Church. All areas west of the border, including western Karelia and southern Finland, came under the control of Sweden and the Roman Catholic Church. The new border thus divided the people of Karelia between two kingdoms, religions, and cultures.

Under the rule of Sweden, Swedish law and the Scandinavian social system were established. The Finns enjoyed full political rights. In 1362, they were given the right to participate in the elections of the king through the Finnish body of *lagmän* (LAG-men), now known as Eduskuntar (EH-dus-koon-tah). In the sixteenth century, a legislative assembly representing four groups—the nobility, clergy, burghers, and farmers—was set up, known as the Diet of the Four Estates.

Gustavus Adolphus ruled over Sweden, and Swedish Finland, from 1617 until his death in 1632.

SWEDEN'S GREAT POWER

In 1611, Gustavus II Adolphus was crowned king of Sweden and its territories, including Swedish Finland. This marked the beginning of Sweden's Great Power period (1611—1721), during which Gustavus II engaged in near constant warfare and increased expansionist policies to extend his country's power and influence. As Swedish control of the Baltic region increased, Finland's border was pushed farther east. By the mid-seventeenth century, Sweden controlled one of the most powerful empires in the world.

Another significant development during this period was the process of "Swedification" in Finland. There was a tightening of administrative control in all aspects of Finnish life to ensure uniformity with Stockholm, Sweden's capital city and its administrative, economic, and cultural hub. The highest posts were filled by Swedes, and the Swedish language grew in importance in Finland.

THE GREAT NORTHERN WAR AND THE GREAT WRATH

More war followed for the Finns after Gustavus II's reign. In 1700, the Great Northern War raged as Russia fought against Swedish control in the region. In 1712, a Russian campaign to capture Finland began. This initial campaign failed, but Russia's Peter the Great called upon his military to attack once again. From 1713 to 1714, Russia successively took over all of Finland, as far as the Åland Islands. During this time, the plague also hit Finland, killing thousands of Finns, including nearly two-thirds of the population of Helsinki. Between the plague and their country's military defeat, this was a trying time for the Finns.

Known as the Great Wrath, this period of Russian occupation ended in 1721 with the Treaty of Uusikaupunki (also known as the Treaty of Nystad). Although Sweden regained control of Finland, it lost Karelia to the Russians. Another war, known as the War of the Hats, broke out between 1741 and 1743. Russia occupied Finland yet again during a period known as the Lesser Wrath. Under the Peace of Turku treaty in 1743, Russia agreed to withdraw its troops in return for more territory, pushing the border farther westward. Sweden ceded the fortified towns of Hamina and Lappeenranta in southeast Finland and the Olavinlinna fortress to Russia.

There were feelings in some quarters that Finland should separate from Sweden. Finnish representatives in the Diet at Stockholm demanded special aid to compensate for their country's suffering during the periods of Russian occupation. This resulted in the introduction of economic reforms and a boosting of Finnish defense over the next few decades. Trade restrictions were removed, a fortress on Suomenlinna was built, and a strong coastal naval fleet was developed. Living standards improved, particularly during the

reign of Gustavus III (1771—1792), and new towns were established. Finnish literature developed, and the Finnish language was accepted in the Diet and for use on currency, and more Finns were appointed to the civil service.

From 1788 to 1790 there was another war with Russia. An attempt among some military officers to separate Finland from Sweden found little support. However, this secessionist attempt was to influence Russia's actions in a war from 1808 to 1809 when, instead of returning occupied territory to Sweden, the Russians held on to Finland, making it a buffer zone with its own diet and administration.

AUTONOMOUS GRAND DUCHY

In 1809, the Finns declared their loyalty to Russian czar Alexander I at a session of the Finnish diet held in the city of Porvoo. The czar became the great duke of Finland, personally overseeing the affairs of Finns. In return for the Finns' loyalty to him and the Russian Empire, Alexander I pledged that he would allow them to continue practicing their Evangelical Lutheran faith. He also promised to guarantee their constitutional rights.

Although Finland was included within the Russian Empire, it became a self-ruling grand duchy that was allowed to continue its traditions and institutions. The czar was the constitutional monarch and was represented by a governor-general. The highest government body was the Senate, made up of Finns who still maintained their Diet of the Four Estates. The Finns also had their own representative at the court of Saint Petersburg who could personally present matters concerning Finland to the czar.

To weaken the influence of Sweden, the czar encouraged building and development in Finland, and Helsinki was made the new capital. The system of roads and canals was improved. Elegant buildings went up to beautify the city.

The period of autonomy gave rise to a new Finnish national consciousness. Finnish literature developed, and there was a movement to promote Finnish as an official language alongside Swedish. During the reigns of Alexander III (1881—1894) and Nicholas II (1894—1917), questions were raised about Finland's autonomous status by the extremist Pan-Slavist group in Russia. The Finns were no longer divided by language, but by their outlook on Russia.

The Russo-Japanese War (1904—1905), in which Russia was defeated, resulted in unrest that extended to Finland, forcing the czar to liberalize his rule. This led to radical parliamentary reform in Finland in 1906, with a new single-chamber parliament replacing the Diet of the Four Estates. Universal suffrage was introduced, and the right to vote was extended to women—a first in Europe.

However, this did not prevent another wave of Russian oppression from taking place from 1908 to 1914, resulting in the "Russification" of the Senate. Finland's autonomy was restored during the Russian Revolution of 1917. Later that year, Finland managed to break completely free from Russian rule.

INDEPENDENCE-AND WAR

After the socialist Bolsheviks gained power of Russia in October 1917, they declared that all Russian territories had the right to rule themselves and to decide to secede from the Russian Empire. The Finnish parliament announced the same day that it would take over power in Finland temporarily. Then, on December 6, 1917, Finland's parliament voted to approve its independence. However, the country itself remained divided. Urban workers and rural farmers felt sympathy with the new socialist government in Russia and wanted to retain Russian ties; they were called the Reds. The Swedish-speaking middle and upper classes, however, rejected socialism; they became known as the Whites. In January 1918, the Reds gained control of the Social Democratic Party (SDP) and began their own Russian-style revolution, taking over Helsinki and southern Finland. Those sympathetic to the Whites fled to Vaasa in Ostrobothnia, where a White government was set up to control northern and central Finland.

In the civil war that erupted, the Whites received assistance from Imperial Germany, with which they had close ties. In May 1918, the Whites, under General Carl Gustaf Mannerheim, won a major battle in Tampere that ended the civil war. Russia pulled out its troops from Finland. Germany then tried to move in to firmly establish its sphere of influence.

However, Mannerheim did not favor strong German links and instead moved to forge ties with the Allied forces. Mannerheim, who became Finland's head of state in December 1918 and held the title of regent, ratified the constitution on July 17, 1919, and Great Britain and the United States finally recognized Finland's independence. K. J. Ståhlberg was elected the first president of the Finnish republic that same year. In 1920, Finland and Russia normalized relations by signing the Peace of Tartu.

The Finnish constitution was a compromise between the republican and the monarchist camps. It gave the president much of the power wielded by the head of state under the previous constitution. Responsible for foreign policy, he was also made commander in chief of the armed forces and given the power to dissolve parliament. The Finnish parliament was kept busy passing legislation in the first years of the new republic. Laws were passed introducing compulsory education and military service, freedom of speech and worship, freedom to form societies, and land reform.

There was a period of healing when Ståhlberg passed an amnesty act that granted pardon to those convicted of leading the Reds. The civil war wounds were further eased when the SDP was allowed to take part in elections in 1919; it later became the largest party in parliament. From 1926 to 1927, the Social Democrats went on to form the government. In 1929, the anticommunist Lapua movement was born, patterned after the Italian Fascists, a group that encouraged militarism and nationalism. The Lapua movement—which had wide support among peasants, who had suffered greatly during the worldwide Great Depression—carried out an armed revolt in 1932, but it was squashed and later outlawed.

In the meantime, the Soviet Union, anxious to bolster the defense of Leningrad, demanded that Finland give up some of its territory and allow a Soviet base to be built on the Hanko Peninsula. Finland refused. In August 1939 the Soviet Union and Germany secretly signed a nonaggression act that ensured German neutrality when the Soviet Union later attacked Finland in November.

Finnish soldiers, next to their skis, are poised to fight during the Winter War.

Although Finland was ill-equipped and fought alone in the Winter War (1939—1940) that ensued, it managed to survive for three and a half months. The war ended with the Peace of Moscow, signed in March 1940. Finland gave up the Karelian Isthmus and the outer islands of the Gulf of Finland to the Soviets, who acquired a base on Hanko.

Finnish fears of Soviet intervention grew worse when the Baltic states were forcibly made part of the Soviet Union in August 1940. Isolated from the West and with Sweden remaining neutral, Finland leaned toward Germany. So when Adolf Hitler invaded the Soviet Union in June 1941, the Finns followed suit in what became known as the Continuation War (1941—1944). Finland occupied Eastern Karelia on the other side of the border, with plans to annex it. However, there was no alliance with Germany and the Finns did not take part in the siege of Leningrad. Still, Great Britain, then an ally of the Soviet Union, declared war on Finland.

The Soviets launched a massive counterattack. Helsinki was bombed, and heavy fighting broke out on the isthmus. Finland withdrew from the war a year before Germany fell in 1943. In September 1944 an armistice was declared in Moscow with terms dictated by the Soviets. Finland returned to its 1940 border in Eastern Karelia and, in place of Hanko, the Porkkala Peninsula was leased to the Soviets for fifty years. Finland also agreed to pay war reparations and reduce the size of its army. German troops in Lapland refused to leave, and the Finns had to force them out in a bitter battle that ended in the spring of 1945.

Finland suffered greatly from the Continuation War, with 65,000 dead and 158,000 wounded. Homes had to be found for 423,000 Eastern Karelians who chose to cross over the border to Finland rather than stay under Soviet rule. Despite the outcome, Finland was the only country on the losing side not to be occupied by foreign troops. This was thanks to Mannerheim, the former head of state and regent, who had been appointed the commander in chief of the armed forces in November 1939, a position he held during the Winter War and the Continuation War. At the end of the Continuation War, Mannerheim was appointed president of the Finnish republic. However, he resigned in 1946 because of poor health and was succeeded by Juho K. Paasikivi, who pursued a policy of reconciliation with the Soviet Union.

"When reading articles on Finland in American and other Western publications, I have found that to many foreign observers Finland seems to be a puzzling phenomenon. To some, the existence of an independent neutral state, a Western democracy, next door to the Soviet Union, maintaining its freedom in friendship with, not in defiance of, its powerful neighbor, appears in itself to be a paradox. In any case, none of the conventional labels of international politics quite fits the position of Finland. As a result it is usually described as 'exceptional.' But an exception from what?"
—Ralf Törngren, in *Foreign Affairs*

In 1948, Finland signed the Treaty of Friendship, Cooperation, and Mutual Assistance with Moscow in which it agreed to prevent any attack on the Soviet Union through Finnish territory. Finland's aim to remain outside great power conflicts became the cornerstone of the Paasikivi line in foreign policy.

Over the years, Finnish external relations began to stabilize. Finland paid off its war debt on time—the only country involved in World War II to do so. As payment was in the form of industrial goods, Finland had to reorganize its production structure. Machinery was rebuilt and the process of industrialization sped up. This paid off in the long run as it resulted in the rapid economic development of the country. Finland completed its war payments in 1952.

In 1956, the Soviets ended their fifty-year lease of Porkkala naval base early and returned it to Finland. The same year, Finland was accepted into the United Nations and the Nordic Council. In 1956, Urho Kekkonen became president and actively pursued Finland's policy of neutrality.

FINLAND POST-WORLD WAR II

Finland flourished in the years following World War II, and its economy grew rapidly, allowing its population one of the highest standards of living in the world. In 1991, the country experienced a brief but intense period of depression where its public debt increased to around 60 percent of its gross domestic product (GDP). The depression ended in 1993.

In 1995, together with Austria and Sweden, Finland became a member of the European Union (EU). It was another historic moment for Finland when it, together with eleven other EU member states, bid farewell to its own currency—in Finland, the markka (MARK-kah)—in favor of the euro on January 1, 2002.

In February 2000, Finland elected its first female president, Tarja Halonen. In March of the same year, it adopted a new constitution. In May 2002, a bill to construct a fifth nuclear power plant, the first in the country in thirty years and the first in western Europe since 1991, was narrowly passed by the Finnish parliament. The move caused the Green League to opt out of the ruling government coalition in protest.

URHO KEKKONEN: ARCHITECT OF FINLAND'S MODERN DESTINY

In the 1950s, as Finland emerged from the shadows of the Soviet Union and took charge of its own destiny, there was one man who helped chart its future: Urho Kekkonen. He was a key figure in rebuilding the economy and maintaining the course of neutrality advocated by Paasikivi, a stand that became known as the Paasikivi-Kekkonen Line. It was a policy that the country followed for the next two decades, allowing it to be friendly with nations in both the North Atlantic Treaty Organization and the Warsaw Pact. He was one of the architects of the modern Finnish state and a very shrewd politician. Kekkonen was Finland's longest-serving president, from 1956 to 1981, and was previously prime minister for two terms, from 1950 to 1956. He was succeeded by Mauno Koivisto, who also adopted the "active neutrality" stance.

Finland elected its first female prime minister, Anneli Jäätteenmäki, in 2003, but after only two months in office, she resigned over a scandal involving political leaks. In January 2006, Tarja Halonen was reelected as president for a second term. Sauli Väinämö Niinistö has been president since 2012, the first conservative president elected since 1956.

Finland's economy was again tested following a global economic crisis in 2008. Although its economy is still recovering and unemployment remains high at nearly 10 percent, Finland remains an economically prosperous and politically stable country.

INTERNET LINKS

news.bbc.co.uk/2/hi/europe/country_profiles/1032683.stm
This timeline from the BBC covers key moments in Finland's history.

finland.fi/life-society/main-outlines-of-finnish-history
The Finnish Ministry for Foreign Affairs provides a comprehensive overview of the country's history, with links to other interesting articles.

GOVERNMENT

The Presidential Palace overlooks Market Square in Helsinki.

3

TODAY, FINLAND IS A DEMOCRATIC republic that is governed by its parliament, the Council of State, and the prime minister. But Finland's system of self-rule is relatively young. From the Middle Ages until 1809, the country was ruled by Sweden. During this time, Finland was part of the Swedish Empire and was ruled according to Swedish traditions and by Swedish institutions.

After 1809, Finland became part of the Russian Empire as an autonomous grand duchy, meaning that it was ruled over by the grand duke, who was the Russian czar. This lasted more than one hundred years until 1917, when Finland cut ties with Russia and entered into a period of civil war. The country emerged from these tensions over its future as a sovereign republican state. Today, Finland's government is lauded for the social and economic policies it has implemented, which provide a high quality of life for its citizens.

In 1907, Finland became the first country in the world to elect women to parliament. That year, nineteen out of the two hundred seats in parliament were won by women, one of whom was feminist and former servant Miina Sillanpää, who would remain in office for forty years.

Finland took eighty years to overhaul its 1919 constitution. Why did it take so long? The answer is simply because there was no pressure or need to do so, especially when the Finnish system allowed the use of exceptive laws to make amendments to its constitution to suit the times.

In 1995 some changes were made to the constitution pertaining to basic rights. It was around this time, especially with Finland's integration into the European Union (EU), that the process of significant constitutional reform began. After all, most of the EU member states' constitutions were contained in one single constitutional act, whereas Finland's constitution had several acts. Also, there was a need to streamline procedures in keeping with those of other EU member states.

"Women who are empowered, and able to realize their full potential, are an incredible force in taking whole nations forward, and in contributing to their well-being."
—Finnish Minister for International Development Pekka Haavisto

FINLAND'S NEW CONSTITUTION

Finland was governed under the constitution it adopted while still an autonomous grand duchy until March 1, 2000. However, between 1919 and 2000, many reforms were made, including the introduction of the direct popular election of the president in 1991. The new constitution took the form of a government bill that sets out the rights of citizens and the structure of the Finnish government.

Finland is a parliamentary democracy; the constitution guarantees the rights of Finnish citizens—who are considered equal before the law—with individual rights and political freedoms enshrined. Ultimate power is in the hands of the people, who are represented by the Eduskuntar, which is the parliament.

The constitution spells out the separation of powers among the parliament, the government, and the judiciary. Legislative power is essentially the domain of the parliament, which also approves state finances. Governmental power is in the hands of the Council of State, comprising the prime minister and ministers for various government departments, as well as the chancellor of justice, who is an ex-officio member. The prime minister, who is elected by parliament, chooses his or her own cabinet ministers, but all ministers have to be formally appointed by the president. Judicial power is vested in the independent courts of law, the Supreme Court, and the Supreme Administrative Court.

There are two hundred members of parliament, and they are elected by direct vote for a period of four years. However, the constitution gives the president the right to dissolve parliament before the end of four years and to declare fresh elections. The new constitution allows for twelve to eighteen electoral districts or constituencies from which members are elected to parliament. The autonomous Åland Islands have their own constituency represented by one member.

THE PRESIDENT OF FINLAND

Before the adoption of the new constitution in 2000, the president of Finland was vested with great power over governance. In fact, the president had so much power that it was often said that Finland was one of the few monarchies left in Europe—which compared the president's rule to that of a king. Today, the president shares his or her responsibilities with the prime minster. The president is still responsible, however, for foreign policy and national security and acts as commander in chief of the nation's armed forces. Presidential authority in domestic politics is also much more limited than it used to be, with the prime minister now taking charge.

Finnish president Sauli Niinistö was elected in 2012.

Still, the post of president is regarded as prestigious. The president wields considerable power on official appointments and is the ultimate decision-maker on pardons. He or she also retains the right to declare elections, to call for emergency sessions of parliament and preside over its opening and closing (but can no longer dissolve parliament if the prime minister has not made such a proposal), and to block legislation by applying his or her temporary right of veto.

RESULTS OF THE APRIL 2015 GENERAL ELECTION

Name of party	Percentage of votes	Parliamentary seats
Centre Party	21.1	49
Finns Party	17.6	38
National Coalition Party	18.2	37
Social Democratic Party	16.5	34
Green League	8.5	15
Left Alliance	7.1	12
Swedish People's Party	4.8	9
Christian Democrats	3.5	5
For Åland in Parliament	0.37	1
Total (turnout 66.9 percent)	100	200

Source: Finnish Ministry of Justice

In 1992, Finland applied for membership to the European Economic Community.

The president presides over the Council of State, attending the ordinary sessions, when government decisions are made on legislative matters. During these sessions, the president makes a formal decision on the legislative bills to be put before parliament or whether to sign acts that have been passed by parliament. The president is not obligated to take into consideration the views of the prime minister or the majority of the Council of State, but in practice he or she usually does. All other meetings of the Council are conducted by the prime minister.

FINLAND'S CABINET

The Council of State is Finland's cabinet, the body that oversees the country's government. The Council of State is appointed by the president, although the prime minister manages its day-to-day operations. The current Council of State was appointed in 2015 by President Sauli Niinistö and is a center-right coalition. All cabinet members must be native-born Finns, and the Council can be dissolved at any moment with a vote of no confidence.

On March 1, 2012, Sauli Niinistö was elected president of Finland. Previous to his presidency, Niinistö was minister of finance and speaker of the parliament. As the National Coalition Party candidate, Niinistö is Finland's first conservative president since 1956. He won against the Green League candidate with 62.6 percent of the vote in the second round of voting. Previously, Niinistö had ran against Tarja Halonen, the incumbent president, in 2006. She won by 3.6 percent in an incredibly close race.

Tarja Halonen

In order for political parties to submit candidates for the election, they must give proof of having more than twenty thousand supporters. The president must be a native-born Finn. The party must also have had at least one member of parliament elected in the most recent parliamentary election.

The election itself consists of two rounds. In the first round, if one candidate were to receive more than half the vote, he or she would automatically win. If this is not the case, which it normally isn't, the second round of voting begins. The two candidates who won the most votes in the previous round are presented, and the one with the most votes wins the presidency.

All Finnish citizens above the age of eighteen have the right to vote. Once elected, the president takes office on March 1 for a six-year term. The president can serve for only two consecutive terms.

Each ministry has its own area of responsibility and is usually headed by a minister, though some ministries are headed by two. There are currently fourteen ministers in the Council of State, excluding the prime minister. The Council decides on important state affairs. Many of the ministries have internal boards where senior civil servants meet regularly to take care of key operational issues concerning the ministry. Issues concerning more than one ministry would be discussed by the ministers, and strategic issues concerning the entire country would be addressed by the Council.

MUNICIPAL GOVERNMENT

For hundreds of years, Finland was divided into six administrative provinces: Åland, Eastern Finland, Lapland, Oulu, Southern Finland, and Western Finland. Each province had a governor who was appointed by the president. In 2010, this system of provinces was abolished. In its place, two agencies have been established: the Centers for Economic Development, Transport, and the Environment and the Regional State Administrative Agencies. There are six Regional State Administrative Agencies in addition to the government of Åland: Southern Finland, Southwestern Finland, Western and Inland Finland, Eastern Finland, Northern Finland, and Lapland. These agencies are primarily tasked with local law enforcement. There are also a total of fifteen Centers for Economic Development, Transport, and the Environment, which are responsible for business and industry, cultural activities, environment and natural resources, and transportation and infrastructure.

The country is further divided into municipalities representing the local level of administration, which oversee community services such as schools and water supplies. Finland has 317 municipalities, of which 107 are cities.

Municipal governments have extensive powers as they are self-governing entities. They are responsible for the administration of their localities, with some funds being provided by the central government, although the municipalities can levy taxes to raise money.

The highest office in local government is the municipal council, which is a decision-making body. The members, numbering thirteen to eighty-five depending on the population of the municipality, are elected directly by residents every four years. The councils vote for their own chairmen. Members of the executive committee—the municipal board—are also elected by the councils every two years. Administrative functions are carried out by statutory and voluntary committees appointed by the councils.

The municipal or town manager holds the highest office in local government. He is appointed by the municipal council and is answerable to the municipal board.

The Åland archipelago, comprising over 6,500 islands and skerries, lies sandwiched between Sweden and Finland. Only 65 islands are inhabited, and they support a total population of some 26,800. The capital and only large town is Mariehamn.

The demilitarized Åland Islands enjoy a special position for historical reasons. Since 1856, at the time of the Crimean War, the islands were recognized under international law as an unfortified area. Most of its people are traditionally Swedish-speaking.

The islands have been largely autonomous since 1920, a status that was reaffirmed in 1951 and again in 1993, when the Act on the Autonomy of Åland was passed by the parliament of Finland on January 1. The governor is the highest official, and he represents the government of Finland in Åland. The islands also have their own provincial parliament with thirty members who are chosen in a general election every four years. The parliament has to approve any change in, or repeal of, laws of a constitutional nature and legislates on all matters that pertain to Åland.

A government body with up to eight members, headed by a chairman who is elected by parliament, carries out the administration of the Åland Islands. It is assisted by a regional civil service and six departments.

The Åland Islands have enjoyed largely autonomous rule since 1920.

Finland's
parliament in
session in 2010

POLITICAL PARTIES AND
PARLIAMENTARY ELECTIONS

Finland has many active political parties, which often share roles in coalition governments. As of 2016, there were eight officially registered parties represented in Finland's parliament, with four unregistered parties also represented in the legislature. The last parliamentary election was held on April 19, 2015, when the Finns elected two hundred members to parliament.

Given Finland's proportional representation system—a system that deems that all voters merit representation and that all political groups ought to be represented in the legislature according to their strength in the electorate—multiple parties are the norm on the country's political scene, which has resulted in many coalition governments. For example, in 2003, eighteen political parties contested the general election. The Communist Party won fifty-five seats in parliament, with slightly more votes (24.7 percent) than

Of the five Nordic countries—Denmark, Sweden, Norway, Finland, and Iceland—the first three are kingdoms. Finland and Iceland are republics.

However, there are traces of a kingdom style of rule in the Finnish constitution, which gives a great deal of authority to its president. The Finnish president wields considerably greater power than the monarchs of Sweden, Great Britain, and the Netherlands. The Finnish president also has greater tangible power than the presidents of many other republics.

Still, in spite of the president's strong position, Finland is a democratic country in the Nordic tradition.

the Social Democratic Party's fifty-three seats and 22.9 percent share of the vote. The Communist Party formed a three-party governing coalition with the Social Democratic Party and the Swedish People's Party.

On April 19, 2015, the Centre Party won forty-nine seats, followed by the Finns Party with thirty-eight seats, the National Coalition Party with thirty-seven seats, and the Social Democratic Party with thirty-four seats. Because the Centre Party won the most seats, the leader of the party, Juha Sipilä, was responsible for forming the coalition party. The resulting three-party coalition, composed of the Centre Party, the Finns Party, and the National Coalition Party, is more politically conservative than previous governments.

The prime minister is traditionally the chairman of the party with the biggest number of votes won in the general elections. Hence, Juha Sipilä, the leader of the Centre Party and a relative newcomer to Finnish politics, became prime minister on May 29, 2015. Sipilä is a well-respected politician who began his career as an entrepreneur in the telecommunications business. The next parliamentary elections are scheduled for 2019.

COURT SYSTEM

According to Finland's constitution, in the case of a dispute, every citizen has the right to be heard in court without an untimely delay. Finland has

FINLAND'S MULTIPARTY SYSTEM

Unlike in the United States, in Finland many political parties vie for votes during a general election. This means that it is often very difficult for one political party to dominate the government. In fact, in Finland's history, nearly every government in modern times has been a coalition government, which means that one political party shares its power with another party.

There is a long list of political parties that dominated at one point during Finnish history before disappearing. Many new political parties splinter off from established parties with new platforms, although there are sometimes single-issue parties that campaign on only one issue. The three largest political parties are the Centre Party (CP), the Social Democratic Party (SDP), and the National Coalition Party (NCP). These political parties have dominated the political scene for over fifty years, although always as part of coalition governments. While the more liberal SDP garners its support from the urban working class, white-collar workers, and professionals, the CP typically represents more rural interests. The Conservative NCP has long developed ties with the business community.

One of the latest major political parties to gain large political clout is the environmentalist Green League, which was formed in 1989. The Green League opposes capitalist systems that endanger the environment. From 1995 to 2002, the Green League formed part of the governing coalition.

In 2015, the Finns Party, previously known as the True Finns, gained significant ground. A nationalist party that argues for strong immigration policies, it came in third behind the NC and SDP in a shocking rise in popularity. Some political analysts view the rise of this largely anti-immigration party as a sign of the times, due to an economic downturn and a steady stream of refugees entering the country.

twenty-seven district courts, six courts of appeals, and one Supreme Court. The district courts typically deal with criminal cases and civil matters like divorce or custody proceedings. There are no juries in Finnish courts, and cases are heard by groups of judges. The courts of appeals deal with cases that have already been heard by district courts and are in appeal. The Supreme Court is composed of a president and eighteen judges; it only hears cases that are significant to the system of law in Finland.

Presidents and members of the Supreme Court are appointed by the Finnish president on the recommendation of the courts. Judges of the district courts are appointed by the Supreme Court; the other members are nominated by municipal councils. The highest legal office is that of the chancellor of justice, appointed by the president. The chancellor is also the highest public prosecutor, overseeing the provincial police superintendents, sheriffs, and municipal public prosecutors. He sees to it that government authorities comply with the law and perform their duties. The chancellor attends the meetings of the Council of State and determines the legality of any decisions made.

The Supreme Court of Finland is located in the country's capital, Helsinki.

INTERNET LINKS

europarlamentti.info/en/elections/political-parties/Finland-parties
Information about Finland's political parties can be found on the European Parliament's website.

www.sverigeturism.se/smorgasbord/smorgasbord/society/history/power-period.html
This Swedish site provides information about the Great Power Period in English.

ECONOMY

The markaa was Finland's currency until the introduction of the euro in 2002.

4

FINLAND'S ECONOMY HAS traditionally been very strong. As a highly industrialized nation, its economic output competes with that of the United Kingdom, Germany, France, and Sweden. The largest economic sector is the service industry, which makes up nearly 73 percent of Finland's economy, followed by manufacturing and refining at just over 31 percent. Main industries in manufacturing include metal and metal products, electronics, machinery and scientific instruments, and pulp and paper.

Finland was forced into rapid industrialization after World War II in order to pay its war debts to the Soviet Union. In a span of just twenty years, Finland's economy transformed. From 1950 to 1974, Finland's average gross domestic product (GDP) grew 5 percent annually. In the 1980s, this number increased to a 6 percent annual growth rate. The first time the country hit dire economic straits in modern times was in the early 1990s, when Finland entered into a recession that resulted in a rise in unemployment. During this time, the value of Finland's currency, the markka, plunged by 25 percent.

Finland seemed to ride out the worst of the global economic crisis, which began in 2008 in the United States and spread to most of Europe

The shopper will find a wide variety of beautifully designed crafts such as ceramics, glassware, and jewelry. The country is also noted for its leather wear, handwoven rugs, and carved wooden objects such as toys.

by 2011. While Finland's economy initially plunged in 2009, it seemed to be making a fast recovery in 2010, 2011, and 2012. At the beginning of 2015, Finland's economy once again contracted, largely due to the decline of Nokia, Finland's largest company. While many experts have faith that Finland will once again rise in the field of high technology, economists are worried about the effect Finland's aging population will have on the country's economy going forward.

AGRICULTURE

Forestry is an integral part of agriculture in Finland, where ample forests produce large amounts of paper and pulp for export. In the summer, Finnish farmers focus on their crops, while during the winter they turn to the forests. Today, with the mechanization of the sector, only 120,000 Finns work in agriculture and forestry, down 30 percent from 2000.

Most of the arable land is concentrated in southern Finland and consists mainly of vegetable gardens and fur farms. The most important crops are wheat, barley, oats, potatoes, rye, sugar beets, and oleiferous plants. From the fur farms come mainly fox pelts, of which Finland is the world's second-largest producer, and mink pelts.

Dairy farming is the most important type of farming in Finland, making up two-thirds of the income earned from farming. At least 33 percent of all farms are dairy farms, while 9 percent are devoted to beef production. Poultry farming is also significant; of the six million poultry in Finland, 74 percent are reared specially for egg production. Finnish exports include eggs, meat, and dairy produce, of which the most famous is Finnish Emmental cheese.

Since the entry of Finland into the EU in 1995, more farms have been converting to organic production, encouraged by subsidies given for such a conversion and compelled by the declining revenue from conventional farming. In 1989, there were only 373 certified organic farms in Finland; the number rose to more than 5,000 in 2002, representing 7.2 percent of all arable land under cultivation in Finland. Farmers are paid a conversion subsidy of 147 euros per hectare for five years, while those already engaged in organic farming receive a grant of 103 euros per hectare, also for five years.

The increase in organic farming is in line with the Ministry of Agriculture and Forestry's strategy launched in October 2001, targeting 15 percent of the arable land under cultivation in Finland to be used for organic farming by 2010. Emphasis is given to the development of organic animal production, organic cereals, horticulture, and food processing. Today, Finland is one of the leading countries in the EU to practice organic farming.

Finland's forests are its most precious natural resource.

FORESTRY

Unlike other Nordic countries, like Norway, which have extensive oil reserves, Finland's forests are its most precious natural resource. Because over 70 percent of the country is covered in forest, it offers ample opportunities for economic development. Pine is the main species in Finnish forests, followed by spruce, birch, aspen, and alder. Timber from these forests is used to make paper, and Finland is the second-largest supplier of paper after Canada. As much as one-quarter of the world's printing and writing paper comes from Finland.

Pulp and paper are produced in this factory.

Paper production continues to be a stable industry for the country. In 2015, paper production increased 6.6 percent from 2014 with 810,000 tons (734,819 metric tons) produced in the fourth quarter. Apart from paper, the forest yields lumber, plywood, pulp, paperboard, panel board, and other paper-related products. Softboard timber, used as roundwood in the sawmill, decreased by 2.7 percent from 2014, with about 10.6 million cubic meters of softwood sawn timber produced. Pulp production increased nearly 2 percent to 7.1 million tons (6.4 million t), while paperboard production amounted to 3.1 million tons (2.8 million t).

Due to improved forest management practices and forest improvement measures, the felling rate of trees is about 20 percent lower than the replacement rate of trees, thus ensuring the sustainability of the forests. In addition, forest protection programs have been put in place by the government. Today, 10 percent of Finnish forests are protected, the highest percentage in all of Europe.

Finland's forests produce high-grade wood. Over 90 percent of all products in its wood industry are exported, accounting for 20 percent of Finland's exports and contributing 8 percent to the country's GDP. Paper and pulp industries top the list.

INDUSTRIAL SECTORS AND ENERGY

Besides timber, paper, and pulp production, Finland's strongest industrial sectors are metals and electronics, which account for nearly one-third of Finland's total exports. Additionally, one-third of the country's industrial workers are employed in these industries. While these industries were initially developed in order to pay back war debts to Russia, Finland has continued to develop these sectors into highly profitable and advanced cornerstones of the Finnish economy.

High-technology sheet steel and copper production are the main sectors of the metal industry, while the mechanical engineering industry turns out automated machines and equipment for the agricultural, forestry, and wood industries; forklifts and trucks; electrical and electronic goods; and other consumer products. Other products include special seagoing vessels such as icebreakers, luxury ocean liners, and oil rigs that are adapted for extreme climatic conditions.

Finland is also well known for its high-tech and innovative industries, such as the production of telephone exchanges, mobile telephones, cars, and electronic consumer goods. The chemical industry has a 10 percent share of total industrial output. Apart from oil refining and fertilizers, the more important branches of the industry include techno-chemical and pharmaceutical production. There is also good demand for products such as textiles, clothing, leather, jewelry, decorative glass, ceramics, furniture, and cutlery. The textile industry, however, has undergone change due to the emergence of cheaper manufacturing bases, like China. Gone are the companies making cotton, wool, and other fabrics. The textile houses that remain, such as Marimekko, concentrate on the design and production of high-end clothing.

The energy industry in Finland is small as there are no fossil fuels in the country. Only 30 percent of total consumption is produced domestically, and the country relies heavily on energy imports from abroad. Traditional sources of domestic energy such as hydroelectric power, wood industry waste, and peat are now supplemented by nuclear power from four stations. A fifth nuclear power plant is being built and is expected to be completed around 2018. If these projects go according to plan, 60 percent of electricity in Finland could soon be produced by nuclear power.

CONSTRUCTION INDUSTRY

During the early high times of the Finnish economy, in the 1960s and 1970s, a construction boom occurred throughout the country. This was due to increased urbanization as people moved to the cities for work. Housing developments were drawn up and built, and roads, railways, canals, and harbors were constructed and updated.

In the 1970s, the construction industry accounted for 9 percent of the GDP, fueled by the building of seventy thousand housing units a year. The 1980s saw a slowdown in housing construction to about half the annual rate, and companies were forced to look abroad for contracts.

Since the 1990s there has been a further shakeup in the construction industry, with several building companies coming under Swedish ownership and others seeking global business opportunities. However, despite the economic crisis of 2008, construction has grown by about 2 percent.

Construction on Helsinki's metro line in 2014

TRANSPORTATION AND COMMUNICATIONS

Although Finland has a relatively small population relative to its size, Finns are spread out across large urban areas. Combined with the cold climates, which can be difficult on building materials, this has burdened Finland's transportation and communications networks while also stimulating their growth.

The country has a network of 48,584 miles (78,189 km) of roads used by 2.8 million vehicles, 90 percent of which are privately owned cars. Road transportation is supplemented by railways. There are 3,642 miles (5,865 km) of tracks; a quarter of these are electrified while the rest use diesel engines. Each major town has its own transportation network. In Helsinki, this includes suburban trains, buses, and the subway.

The Saimaa Canal, which was built in the nineteenth century, gives boats access to the lakes of eastern Finland. Other canals allow people, goods, and timber to be transported along lakes and rivers. Inland waterways, however, have been largely replaced by roads, although shipping is still important between the Baltic and Finnish lake districts.

Finland has a well-developed domestic air network, recognized as one of the best in Europe. There are 148 airports in the entire country, the most important being Helsinki-Vantaa Airport, which handles 90 percent of all scheduled international flights and over ten million passengers a year. More than one hundred scheduled and charter airlines serving sixty destinations operate via Helsinki. The national carrier, state-owned Finnair, has international links to major cities, including in the United States, Japan, and China.

Finland was long a communications powerhouse because of Nokia, once the world's largest producer of cell phones. Nokia sold its mobile devices division in 2014 due to the rise of smartphones and has since focused on telecommunications infrastructure, GPS systems, and acquiring other companies. Many experts have linked the fall of Nokia's mobile devices division to a recent decline in Finland's economy.

Helsinki International Airport served 15.3 million passengers in 2013.

The Finns enjoy a superior, fully digitized telephone network and communications system. Automated telecommunications—instant communications without the need for human intervention—cover the entire country, and landlines are available everywhere, except in the most remote locations. Nearly 92 percent of Finland's population uses the internet, among the highest in the world. Nearly everyone in Finland also owns and uses a mobile phone, with an increase in use in recent years among Finns aged seventy-five to eighty-nine.

TRADE

Foreign trade is essential to the health of Finland's economy. In the early twentieth century, the country's main exports were wood and paper products. This changed in the 1950s, when metal and engineering products sent to the Soviet Union became the chief exports. Today, Finland mainly trades with its partners in the European Free Trade Association (EFTA), which it joined in 1961, and the EU, which it joined in 1995. Finland is a highly integrated country in the global economy, and trading with EU countries makes up 60 percent of

Finland's total trade. Sweden is its largest trading partner in the EU, followed by Germany, Britain, France, and the Netherlands.

Outside the EU, Finland's biggest trading partner is Russia, followed by the United States and Japan. Trade with Russia and other countries from the former Soviet Union declined after the latter's collapse, amounting to only 5 percent of total exports in 1995. This has since risen to nearly 9 percent.

TOURISM

Finnish hotels and tourist accommodations recorded approximately 19.8 million overnight stays by foreign visitors to the country in 2015. Most foreign visitors come from Russia and Sweden, followed by Germany, the United Kingdom, and France. Recently, the amount of Chinese tourists visiting the country has doubled. According to economic forecasts, the tourism industry is poised to grow exponentially over the next several years.

Although most visitors travel by air to Helsinki, many come by ship or car ferry from Sweden, as Helsinki is an overnight journey from Stockholm, the Swedish capital. Summer is the favorite season for travel in Finland, thanks to the warm weather and a full calendar of events, including several music and dance festivals. Lapland is a favorite tourist destination because it offers visitors a chance to experience the great outdoors, and visitors can also pan for gold in many areas. Lapland is also the official home of Santa Claus. Nearly half a million visitors descend on a small village just outside of Rovaniemi in Lapland, close to the Napapiiri, or Arctic Circle, to visit him and his elves at his workshop. Each year, since 1950, letters written by more than six hundred thousand children from all over the world and addressed simply to "Santa Claus, Arctic Circle" have been delivered there.

Flights by Finnair, the national airline, connect Helsinki and the rest of the country to major European cities, the American continents, and Asia, making Finland very accessible. Traveling in Finland is easy, as English is widely spoken.

A NEW CALLING

Nokia was long Finland's biggest success story. In 2010, Nokia remained the leading corporation by sales in Finland, with more than $58.72 billion in sales. When Microsoft bought Nokia's mobile device division in 2014, many thought this was the end of the quintessentially Finnish company. But not so fast.

Despite its recent troubles in the mobile devices sector, Nokia is poised to grow in strength due to investments in new technologies such as virtual reality systems. According to many people in the town of Nokia, this is part of their people's—and their corporation's—strength. Although Nokia gained fame as a producer of mobile phones, it only did this for twenty years. Nokia was long able to adapt to different consumer needs and technologies, and the Finns believe that the company will continue to do so. Virtual reality systems are one avenue that the company has spent funding on, as well as GPS map systems.

INTERNET LINKS

www.bbc.co.uk/news/business-35656150

This BBC article delves into Finland's most recent economic crisis.

www.oecd.org/eco/surveys/economic-survey-finland.htm

The Organization for European Cooperation and Development (OECD) provides data from the 2016 economic survey of Finland.

ENVIRONMENT

Lush forests and grasslands cover much of Finland and have been protected through environmental reform in recent years.

5

FINLAND REGULARLY RANKS among the highest-rated countries for environmental sustainability and conservation. It has been named as a leading country in environmental protection standards by the Global Economic Forum's Environmental Sustainability Index, as well as by studies conducted by Yale and Columbia universities. Finland's strength is due to both its low population density and conservation legislation, as well as the concern for environmental sustainability in all areas of Finnish life.

But it wasn't always like this. In the 1970s, in the face of rapid industrialization, Finland faced many environmental problems, including a rapid loss of forests and biodiversity and air and water pollution. Largely in response to this crisis, the Ministry of the Environment was formed in 1983 to focus on environmental conservation despite Finland's industrial development. Following on the heels of this was the formation of the Green League in 1987, the first major political party in modern Finland's history to develop in response to a perceived need of the Finnish people.

"We depend on nature and the environment for everything. If we allow our forests and lakes to become polluted, our Finnishness will disappear too. The hearts of the Finnish people lie in the lakes and forests. They are our identity, our capital, and riches."
—Matti Arkko, environmental activist

That same year, the Ministry of the Environment published the National Report on Environmental Protection in Finland. In this in-depth report, the ministry outlined problem areas in terms of environmental degradation and solutions to these problems.

Today, Finland enjoys its well-earned reputation as one of the most environmentally conscious countries in the world. The Green League holds important positions in the Finnish government. And many steps have been taken, on local and national levels, to reduce waste, protect important natural resources, increase biodiversity, and cut down on the use of nonrenewable energy. But there is still work to be done.

AIR POLLUTION AND ACID RAIN

As with most industrialized nations, air pollution in Finland has become a major problem due to the pollutants released from factories into the air. While air pollution itself can be devastating for both the environment and for people, who may experience asthma or other breathing problems, it can also lead to even greater health threats, including acid rain. Acid rain occurs when pollutants in the air make rainfall acidic, which causes harm to forests and lakes—and the creatures living there—when it precipitates to earth. During the height of Finland's industrialization, the worst pollutants released into the air were nitrogen and sulfuric acid.

In the past twenty years, through a number of measures to fight air pollution, Finland has significantly reduced harmful emissions from power stations, industrial plants, and motor vehicles. Sulfur emissions, for instance, dramatically dropped by 80 percent from 1980 to 1995. Nitrogen emission was reduced by 10 percent over the same period.

The measures adopted included cutting down on the use of industrial fuel, using more nuclear energy, and improving production methods in the pulp, paper, chemical, and metal industries.

Today, Finns enjoy better air quality than many other Europeans. However, two outstanding issues remain. One is the quality of urban air, which has not improved as rapidly as hoped. The concentration of fine particles from traffic emissions, industrial plants, and power stations still needs to be reduced. The second outstanding environmental issue is acid rain, which cannot be solved by Finland alone; the source of acid rain comes less from Finland than from its neighboring countries, and the issue of cross-border pollution requires international cooperation to resolve.

Syote National Park

In 2002, the Finnish government launched its air pollution control program, laying out a wide range of measures to cut down emissions from traffic, energy production, industry, agriculture, machinery, leisure boats, and the combustion of wood. The program also set maximum annual emission levels for sulfur dioxide, ammonia, nitrogen oxide, and other gases, to be met by 2010. The implementation of this program, which was designed to meet the EU National Emissions Ceilings Directive, involves international cooperation and, when implemented throughout Europe, will help to solve Finland's two outstanding issues.

DEFORESTATION

Finland's famous forests have not only formed much of the country's cultural identity, but they have also served as the backbone of the Finnish economy. While the natural resources provided by these forests have helped the country become a powerhouse in the production of timber, paper, and pulp, this has not been without consequence. In the late twentieth century, the Finnish government grew concerned about deforestation, the loss of biodiversity due to timber and paper production, threats to natural habitats, and environmental sustainability.

To address this, Finland passed the Wilderness Act in 1991. Twelve wilderness areas in Lapland, totaling an area of 1.5 million acres (3.7 million ha), 5 percent of Finland's land area, were designated as protected areas. Since then, more protected areas, including old-growth forests, have been designated.

Waves crash against the rocky shore in Helsinki.

In 1997, a National Action Plan for Biodiversity was drawn up. Its key goal was to protect the country's biodiversity by preventing the depletion of habitats and natural organisms. The plan was revised in 2005. In addition, the Forest Act and the Act on the Financing of Sustainable Forestry were both implemented in 1997 to prevent logging activities in a growing forest and to stipulate a timeframe for regeneration work.

In 1999, the National Forest Program 2010 came into force, aimed at securing employment and income derived from forestry, ensuring the health of forests and biodiversity, and allowing people the right to enjoy recreational pursuits that only forests can offer. This was extended to the Forestry Program of 2015, which continues the mandate of protecting the nation's forests.

The regulatory work of the Ministry of Agriculture and Forestry has enabled Finland to conserve its forests. The rate of deforestation in Finland today is low. It is estimated that Finnish forests have a total stock of 70.6 billion cubic feet (2 billion cubic m) of timber, enough to encircle the entire globe with a wall that is approximately 33 feet (10 m) wide and 16.4 feet (5 m) high. The rate at which the stock is regularly replenished—2.6 billion cubic feet per year (75 million cubic m a year) is higher than the annual rate of harvesting—2.1 billion cubic feet (60 million cubic m)—thus ensuring sustainability. From 1945 to 2015, the growing stock increased by more than 40 percent and the area of protected forests tripled.

WATER PROTECTION POLICIES

Given its high number of lakes and the length of its coastline, it is no surprise that water protection ranks high on Finland's list of environmental goals. Due to a targeted water protection program, water quality across 80 percent of Finland's lakes is rated as excellent or good. Water around industrial sites has also improved in recent years. However, the country's small and shallow bodies of water are more susceptible to pollution, and more work is needed to protect their waters.

To improve the situation, a number of long-term strategies have been adopted. An act on river basin management was passed in 2004. The act called for the creation of plans that served as guidelines on managing river basins to achieve a good state of surface waters and groundwater by 2015.

In 2005, an action plan for the Program for the Protection of the Baltic Sea, also to be implemented by 2015, was approved. The program is aimed at reducing maritime traffic risks, decreasing risks from hazardous substances at sea, protecting biodiversity, and generally increasing awareness on environmental pollution.

A national water protection policy was approved in 2006. The policy identified five water protection targets for 2015: achieving good water quality; combating eutrophication, or excessive nutrient levels in lakes due to land runoff; targeting agricultural emissions; intensified nitrogen removal; and social impacts. Following this program, the European Environment Agency (EEA) rated water quality along Finland's beaches at the highest level in past years, with 84 percent of Finland's coastal waters graded as excellent.

About 10 percent of Finland's lakes are affected by acidification—a low figure considering the vast number of lakes in the country. However, this percentage is also decreasing in large part due to the country's strong water protection policies in recent years.

CONSERVATION EFFORTS

Finland has many important habitats for its flora and fauna, the most important, besides its forests, being the wetlands that surround the country's lake district. Here, there are several birds and other wildlife that are still in danger due to habitat loss, pollution, and hunting. In Finland's 2015 assessment of endangered bird and mammal species, several species were classified as threatened, including the Natter's bat, arctic fox, gray wolf, and European polecat.

Since the 1960s, Finland has introduced a number of protection programs, including drawing up a network of protected areas with different biotopes

"Everyman's right" is the Finnish tradition of public access rights to the country's lands. This means that, even if an area is privately owned, foreigners and Finns alike can use the area freely, as long as they do not damage the environment or disturb others around them.

Everyman's rights include being able to walk, ski, or bike over any land, except if it is a private garden or cultivated area where plants may be damaged; the right to pick wild berries, mushrooms, and flowers anywhere; and the ability to stay for a short period of time in any outside area, as long as you do not disturb residents. This means that Finns can pitch tents in almost any park, forest, or other location for an overnight camping trip.

for wildlife. These include national parks and nature reserves, waterfowl habitats, shorelines, and forest areas.

With an active conservation program, the white-backed woodpecker is off the endangered species list. Finland's conservation efforts have enabled the Saimaa seal population to increase in recent years, although it is still on the highly protected list. The white-tailed eagle has also rebounded thanks to Finland's efforts and, while once on the brink of extinction, today they are a common sight in Finland's skies.

Overall, Finland's nature is clean, according to a recent World Wildlife Fund report. Most of Finland's lakes are pristine, and 50 percent of its peatlands are still in their original state. Many of its forests are untouched, and there are areas in Lapland where few people have been.

WASTE MANAGEMENT

In the past, Finland was known for producing the most municipal waste per capita of all countries in Europe. However, in 2008, the Finnish government approved a new national waste plan for 2016. This followed on the heels of the first national waste plan, which was implemented from 1998 to 2005. Each of Finland's thirteen regional environment centers has its own regional waste plan, as well.

Finland's waste management policy centers on preventing waste, reducing the amount of biodegradable waste and the emission of methane (a greenhouse gas), and increasing the rate of recycling as well as the safe treatment of wastes.

From 2001 to 2010, there was an increase from 465 kilograms per capita to 521 kilograms per capita. However, a dramatic decrease from 2008 to 2010 brought waste per capita back down to 2001 levels. There was a reduction of waste landfilled from 60 percent in 2001 to 45 percent in 2010. Incineration rates rose during this time, while recycling levels stayed stable at 35 percent.

MINISTRY OF THE ENVIRONMENT

Finland's Ministry of the Environment works with the government and parliament to create laws for the sustainable use of natural resources and the environment, protect biodiversity, and promote environmentally conscious communities. The ministry is led by the minister of agriculture and the environment. Its umbrella of influence is the Finnish Environment Institute, which focuses on environmental research and development. Thirteen regional environment centers look after the conservation of nature in their respective areas.

In addition, two other organizations are involved in conservation: Metsähallitus Natural Heritage Services is charged with monitoring and protecting threatened species in the wilderness and in the nature reserves, while the Finnish Forest Research Institute manages the forest research areas in some nature reserves.

INTERNET LINKS

finland.fi/life-society/environmental-protection-in-finland
Find out about Finland's environmental policies and the animals categorized as threatened here.

Finland's Ministry of the Environment
http://www.ym.fi/en
This is the official site for Finland's Ministry of the Environment.

FINNS

Many people think all Finns have blue eyes, fair skin, and blond hair, although this is not true.

THE FINNS MAKE UP A GENETIC
mixture of native-born, historical
immigrants from other countries,
and recent immigrants. While most people
think that the Finns, as Nordic people,
have light eyes, fair skin, blond hair, and
a tall stature, this isn't, of course, always
the case. Rather, Finns today are a proud
mixture of different groups of people and
can have dark hair and dark eyes as well
as the stereotypical physical attributes
that many people typically associate with
Finnish people.

Modern genetic research has shown that nearly 75 percent of Finns'
genome is European in origin, while the remaining 25 percent is Asian
Siberian. Finns today living in the east of the country have more Siberian
genes, while those living toward the south and west of Finland have
more European blood.

ANCIENT HISTORY

While it was originally thought that humans began to migrate into Finland
only after the end of the last ice age, new archaeological discoveries have
questioned this long-held belief. Around 9000 BCE, people speaking early

Finnish languages pushed westward from areas in modern-day Russia and Poland into what is present-day Finland. During the second millennium BCE, these languages began to evolve into separate Finnish and Sami languages. Starting around the first century CE, Baltic and Germanic groups began to settle in the south and southwest of modern-day Finland.

The wave of Swedish settlers began when Sweden embarked on its colonization of Finland around the first millennium CE, starting with the Åland Islands and the island of Gotland and moving into the coastal regions of the Gulf of Finland and the Gulf of Bothnia. Today, Swedish Finns make up 6 percent of the population. They retain their own language and culture but are Finnish citizens. Many others have blended into the ethnic mix that makes up Finnish people today. The Finns consider themselves to be European but also proudly celebrate their unique heritage, diverse ancestry, and language.

A father and son dressed in traditional Sami clothing in Lapland, circa 1900

NATIONAL CHARACTER

Stereotypically, Finns are known for being strong, resilient, and somewhat reserved. Author and historian Zachris Topelius wrote, "[A] Finn is known for his reserve, for his caution. He needs time to relax and get to know people, but when he does, he is a trustworthy friend," in *Finland in the Nineteenth Century*. Of course, not all Finns are the same. However, Finnish banker Kai Heinonen relates this view of Finns to their homeland's past. He states, "Finns are generally suspicious of outsiders because of centuries of isolation. They are also a shy people and until recently not many could speak English, so there was this language barrier with foreigners."

Finns have changed; their reticence and self-deprecating nature have given way to a new self-confidence as Finland enjoys its standing as one of the most "wired" nations in the world, with one of the highest percentages of cell phone and internet usage. Finland gave the world Linux, the first open-source software operating system, which was pioneered by university student Linus Torsvald in 1991. Finland is also the home of Nokia. Finnish youth are highly educated and connected to technology. There are forty-eight personal computers for every one hundred Finns, and there are more internet hosts per capita in Finland than in any other country besides the United States. Access to wireless technology also costs less in Finland than most other countries; internet service in Finland is about 50 percent below the standard rate in the United States, allowing more Finns to take advantage of it.

POPULATION

Finland's population exploded from the mid-eighteenth century until the early twentieth century. During the first population records taken in Finland during the 1750s, just under half a million people lived in Finland at that time. By 1800, that figure had risen to 800,000. Just seventy years later, Finland's population doubled to 1.77 million. It doubled again by 1915. This rapid population growth was largely due to improved medical care and, thus, improved health conditions and a decrease in the death rate.

Since then, Finland's birth rate has declined; the size of the population was 4 million after World War II and 5.5 million in 2016. During the 1980s, the government tried to increase the birth rate by offering incentives and benefits to encourage families to have more children. However, one-child families are still common. Out of the six hundred thousand families with children in 2004, 43 percent had only one child, while 38 percent had two children; families with four or more children made up only 4.8 percent. In the year 2016 the percentage of live births (10.3 percent) to deaths (10.7 percent) resulted in a negative population growth rate.

The negative birth rate has been offset by immigration, which helped to increase the population to .02 percent in 2015 when more than 20,700 immigrants entered Finland. While earlier immigrants came from Russia,

Sweden, and Estonia, most immigrants today enter Finland as refugees fleeing war in Iraq, Afghanistan, Somalia, and Syria.

Apart from a low birth rate, the Finnish population is aging. The proportion of the population under fifteen years of age declined from 30 percent in 1950 to 17.5 percent in 2004, and later to 17.3 by the end of 2005. Ten years later, in 2015, it decreased to 15.8 percent. In contrast, the percentage of the elderly (age sixty-five and above) has doubled during the same period, from 7 percent in the 1950s to 19.8 percent in 2015. The average life expectancy for Finns is among the highest in the world at eighty-one years; the average gender-specific lifespan in the country is eighty-four years for women and seventy-eight years for men.

POPULATION TRENDS

With a population of just under 5.5 million, Finland is the third most sparsely populated country in Europe, following Iceland and Norway. About 85 percent of Finns live in cities and towns, and most of them are concentrated in the southwestern region of the country. Northern Finland is much more sparsely populated. There are only two people every square kilometer in Lapland. The biggest town in Finland is its capital, Helsinki, with more than 550,000 residents, followed by Espoo with 256,000 residents, and Tampere, with just over 200,000 residents.

The country's main towns lie in the south and southwest because of industrialization and the spread of commerce. After World War II, when Finland started to industrialize rapidly and people were freed from farming jobs because of mechanization, workers moved from the inland rural areas to the factories and offices in the southern region around Helsinki. In recent years, however, the migration of people from rural areas has stopped and urban growth has slowed down.

The number of Finns emigrating has also had an influence on population size. It is estimated that about 555,000 Finns have emigrated to Sweden since the end of World War II, though half of them returned to Finland later or moved to another country. Today, nearly 5 percent of the population of Sweden is made up of first- or second-generation Finns. Other popular places for emigration include Norway, Germany, and the United States.

Finnish gypsies form the nation's largest minority ethnic group. Most of them live in the southern part of the country, where they continue to practice their age-old customs.

THE SAMI PEOPLE

The Sami people are the indigenous people who inhabit the northern areas of Finland, as well as northern Norway, Sweden, and Russia. There is a total population of approximately 137,477 Sami today. However, the Finns and Sami have intermarried for hundreds—if not thousands—of years, meaning that a large population of Finland can trace their ancestors to Sami heritage. Some of these people of mixed Sami-Finnish heritage identify as Finns, while others identify primarily as Sami. Unfortunately, the Sami have long experienced discrimination across the Nordic countries. While Finland has laws in place to preserve Sami heritage and languages, activists claim that the country has also largely taken over the Sami's ancestral land without compensating them. This was disastrous for the Samis, who have long lived off the land as hunters, gatherers, and reindeer herders.

A mother and daughter show off their traditional Sami clothing.

Some Sami people continue to live off the land, much as their ancestors did, and about 10 percent of Sami are still nomadic reindeer herders. They are experts at hunting and fishing, and they raise large herds of reindeer, which they depend on for a living. Reindeer are used to pull their sledges and transport their goods; the reindeer also provide milk and meat, and their skins are used to make clothes and tents The antlers of the reindeer are highly prized and are carved into pieces of sculpture. The Sami sell souvenirs made from reindeer fur and bone carvings at roadside stalls along the northern highways. While valuing their traditional ways of life and arts, today's Sami are also open to modern technology and innovations: cars, mobile phones, the internet, and other features of the modern world are as common among Sami as they are among Finns.

The traditional dwelling of the Sami is a tent that is shaped like a Native American tepee. Called a *goahti* (GO-ah-tee), it comprises a pole frame covered with reindeer skins. Inside, skins are also used to keep the ground warm, and in winter, woven wool rugs keep the tent insulated. Some Sami still use a goahti seasonally, particularly when following reindeer herds from their spring to summer grazing areas.

The Sami have a colorful traditional costume that is green, red, and blue. It is worn with an embroidered cap. The upturned moccasin-like shoes that they wear in the winter are made from reindeer fur; so are their gloves, leggings, and coats. Hay is placed inside the boots and sometimes in the gloves for warmth.

Rovaniemi is the gateway to Lapland. It has a Sami village where the Sami way of life and customs are demonstrated to visitors. One custom is a traditional Sami welcome, which involves drinking reindeer milk from a small ceramic cup, then having the milk poured down one's back!

TRADITIONAL FINNISH DRESS

The traditional Finnish dress, consisting of a vest, skirt or trousers, and shirt, dates from the sixteenth and seventeenth centuries. It was revived during the nineteenth century as a symbol of national pride. Today, the Finnish national dress, called *kansallispuvu*, is typically only worn during national celebrations or during folk dances or festivals.

The dress for men consists of a linen or cotton shirt, a vest, and a wool or cotton jacket teamed with a pair of trousers or knee breeches made from wool or chamois leather. Black leather shoes are worn with gray or black socks. A scarf is wrapped around the collar and tied with a single knot, and a belt with key hook and knives completes the look.

The dress for women consists of a skirt and apron with a bow tied at the back. The top is a laced bodice. A scarf, tied into a triangle, may be worn underneath the bodice or on top of it.

A headdress is usually worn. It can be a cap with a hard crown and lace, a white soft cap with lace, or an embroidered version of either. A key hook hanging from the waistband and a pair of black shoes add the finishing touch.

There are craft schools that teach the making of the Finnish traditional dress to those who are interested.

Dancers, dressed in traditional Finnish clothing, celebrate the midsummer festival.

INTERNET LINKS

www.finlandia.edu/about/our-finnish-heritage
Find more about the attitude of *sisu* here.

www.listal.com/list/100-greatest-finns
A list of the most famous Finns in history can be found here.

LIFESTYLE

Helsinki residents enjoy a street festival in 2016.

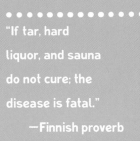

7

THE FINNS OFTEN TOP THE LIST OF standards of living and well-being. While they have a slightly smaller average disposable income, about 70 percent of Finns have a paying job, which is above average for all countries in Europe. Finns typically spend about 20 percent of their income on housing. About 73 percent of Finns own their own homes, and about 16 percent live in housing provided by the government.

The generous housing programs were adopted by the government in the 1950s, among many other social programs established that have increased the overall quality of life in the country. In recent years, the cost of housing has greatly increased in Finland, although housing in Finland still costs less compared to other Nordic countries.

Since the deregulation of the financial sector in 1995, 90 percent of housing loans are principally administered by banks. Today, following the Eurozone economic crisis, housing loan interest rates are historically low. The average housing interest rate was 1.27 percent as of December 2015, among the lowest rates of most countries. This has successfully jump-started the housing market, and more Finns are buying houses in recent years than before.

TRADITIONAL AND CONTEMPORARY ROLES

Traditional Finnish family roles have changed in recent years.

As in other countries, rapid modernization has changed the structure of the Finnish family itself. Whereas in the past, young Finnish couples would wait to get married before living together, today cohabitation is common. Gender roles have similarly changed. Prior to World War II, it was common for women to stay at home and raise children while men were the breadwinners. Today, thanks in part to generous parental leave programs, there are many more dual-income households in Finland.

The typical Finnish family spends about 13 percent of its combined household income on food. Cultural activities and recreation absorb another 11 percent of the family income, while transport accounts for 12 percent. Virtually every household has a television set and one or more cell phones, while 82 percent of Finnish households own a personal computer.

As in many countries around the world, the traditional roles of men and women in the household have evolved into one of partnership, with family burdens being shared between husband and wife and critical decisions like the kind of schools their children attend or where the family should live being made jointly. Increasingly, men are getting more involved in bringing up their children and doing household work.

With the rise of internet usage, the traditional family lifestyle has also undergone changes; the increasing use of technology has created social barriers, with some families interacting less often because children and adults spend more time on their computers or mobile devices rather than interacting with family members.

A DAY IN THE LIFE

With more families sharing domestic chores and wages, it is becoming increasingly common for both partners in a family to share household chores. Today, about 78 percent of men and 73 percent of women work outside of the home. Women and men prepare quick breakfasts for themselves and their children before seeing their children off to school. Lunch at school is typically served between 11:00 and 11:30 a.m. Work lunches are typically taken between 11:00 a.m. and 2:00 p.m. and last between one and two hours. Depending on when parents arrive home from work, dinner is typically served between 5:00 and 7:00 p.m. It is usually simple since, during the weekdays, there isn't much time to prepare elaborate meals.

Many Finns enjoy hobbies such as berry foraging or mushroom picking.

The weekends are important for family time. Much time is spent enjoying the great outdoors—going for walks, jogging, or bird-watching. During the summer, many families spend weekends at their lakeside summer homes fishing, sailing, having an outdoor barbecue, or enjoying their sauna, followed by a dip in the crystal-clear waters of the lake. In the fall, they go into the woods to pick berries and mushrooms or to admire the changing colors of the trees. During the winter, they go ice-skating or skiing. There is more time over the weekend to cook elaborate family meals.

FINNISH WOMEN

Finnish women enjoy more rights compared to women in many other countries. In 1906, Finland was the second country in the world (after New Zealand) and the first country in Europe to grant voting rights to women. This early focus on gender equality has continued today. Finnish women hold prominent positions in government and business, they are highly educated, and they have just as many opportunities as men to work outside of the home. When they are married, most Finnish women keep their maiden

Finnish women have long enjoyed freedoms for which women in other parts of the world struggled.

The Equality Act of 1987 makes gender discrimination in the workplace a violation of Finnish law.

names in addition to their married names. While 73 percent of women work outside of the home, Finnish women still only make eighty-one cents to every dollar that a man earns. However, the government has set guidelines that require businesses that employ more than thirty employees to guarantee a gender-equality salary plan.

Finland is ranked number one in the world for its family leave programs. Current labor laws grant women eleven months of paid maternity leave, of which the first three months is termed maternity leave. The remaining eight months is termed parental leave, and parents can choose whether they want the mother or father to care for the child at home. A parental allowance is also given, although for the first eighteen months this allowance goes only to the mother, after which it is applicable to either the father or mother, depending on who decides to apply for parental leave. At the end of this period, there is a further entitlement of three years' unpaid leave from work, and the employer is obliged to keep the job open and available. In addition, a child home-care allowance is available until the youngest child turns three years of age. In recent years, the government has focused on providing "rainbow families," or non-heterosexual families, with the same rights and privileges as heterosexual families.

Husbands are entitled to a paid paternity leave of about three weeks. Every woman is given a "mother's box," which is a maternity gift from the government, upon the delivery of a child. The box includes a mattress that can act as a bed for the baby, a toy, and a gift pack of children's clothes, blanket, creams, a hairbrush, and winter clothes. Cash is given if the mother prefers this, although the amount would be less than what is usually given in kind. All postnatal care is free.

The Finns enjoy one of the best educational systems in the world, as well as being a country with one of the best standards of life. But, despite this, many young Finns are leaving their country and seeking opportunities elsewhere. According to recent statistics, 9,600 Finns between the ages of twenty and thirty-four left the country in 2015, an increase of about 1,000 people from 2010. However, the largest emigration took place in 2011, when close to 11,000 Finns left the country during the height of the economic crisis. Experts state this is due to EU laws in which it is easy to explore different countries to live and work there. Many Finns eventually move back home.

MARRIAGE

Typically, marriages in Finland occur in the church, whether or not the couple are active churchgoers. Most couples choose to marry in the spring or summer to enjoy the beautiful weather during their celebration. As of 2017, same-sex marriage is legal everywhere in Finland.

Traditionally, the man would ask the father of his wife-to-be for her hand in marriage. The dinner celebration, which was held after the church wedding, would then be hosted by the bride's parents at their home or in a restaurant. These days, the couple is likely to defray the costs or share them with their parents. The Finns believe that whoever has his or her hand uppermost on the knife when cutting the wedding cake will be the "boss" of the family. This also explains the custom of the bride and bridegroom rushing to be the first to step on each other's foot!

After the cutting of the cake, the dancing begins. The new couple has the first dance; the father of the bride then dances with the bride, while the bridegroom dances with his mother-in-law.

To mark the marriage, the parents of the bride also present gifts to the new couple. And on their first day as husband and wife, the bridegroom presents his wife with a gift of jewelry. In the past, the custom was for the bridegroom to give his bride a decorated wooden spindle so that his bride could weave clothes for the family. These days, if a spindle is given, it is used more as a decoration for the new home.

CHILDREN

The birth of children is greeted with joy in Finland, as it is in most countries in the world. Most Finnish women give birth in hospitals today. Home births do occur, but they are not encouraged by the Finnish state and are not covered by public health services.

When the mother and baby return home from the hospital, friends and relatives visit, bringing food, clothes, and other presents for the baby. A kind of pastry known as *rinkelli* (RING-kel-li) is served with coffee and is also traditionally brought by visitors. One to three months later, a christening ceremony is held in the home. The baby usually wears a long dress made of lace, on which the names of those who have worn the same dress for christenings are embroidered. This may include the baby's mother, father, or siblings.

The Finns traditionally leave their babies out on the open balconies of their homes to "get used to the fresh air," even during

As in most other countries in the world, the birth of children in Finland is a joyous occasion.

winter. They are warmly wrapped up, of course; it is believed that this makes them healthy.

Finland's infant mortality rate of two deaths in every one thousand live births is one of the lowest in the world. Many experts link this low infant mortality rate with Finland's policies toward childbirth and its equal treatment of all babies born in the country.

EDUCATIONAL SYSTEM

The compulsory educational system in Finland lasts for nine years, from the ages of seven to sixteen. During this time, attendance is mandatory. Finland's education system relies on equal treatment of all students; homeschooling is rare, and stronger students are mixed in with weaker students and are expected to help those who need it.

After completing this comprehensive education, students can choose to attend upper secondary schools or to enroll in vocational school for three additional years. After this, students can decide whether or not they want to continue to university or a polytechnic school. Tuition is free in both vocational and academic secondary schools, and students are provided with free health care, free lunch, and subsidized housing. However, students are expected to buy their own books and study materials.

Following this secondary education, students in traditional universities or polytechnic schools can obtain a bachelor's degree or continue on to achieve a master's or doctorate degree. Some universities provide

Finland is known for its comprehensive education system.

professional degrees as well. Finland has twenty universities, of which ten are multidisciplinary, four are art academies, three offer economics and business administration courses, and three specialize in technology. There are twenty-nine polytechnic schools in the country. Adult learners are also encouraged to continue their education. Finland's Open University encourages students to enroll in individual classes without having a student status. Costs are low, at approximately 60 euros per class. The government's free education program is also a way in which Finland promotes lifelong learning. State-funded and independent educational institutes work together to provide education to Finns who want to continue to learn later in life although they may not have had a traditional educational background.

EARLY EDUCATION

Early education starts young in Finland. As part of the maternity package given to each family, the Finnish government provides three books, one for each parent and a baby book for the child, to foster an early love of education. Universal childcare is available for children ages eight months to five years old. The government also pays mothers a stipend to stay at home and teach their children for the first three years. Care workers occasionally visit these homes to make sure that the atmosphere is appropriate for the needs of the child. While preschool is not mandatory in Finland, almost everyone uses it. Approximately 90 percent of all six-year-olds attend preschool.

The Ministry of Social Affairs and Health and the local authorities work together to place young children of working parents into daycare centers and homes. Since 2001, it was decreed that all children had the right to preschool education and that this would be provided, free of charge, within the framework of daycare, wherever possible.

A LOVE OF READING

Some are surprised that Finland has one of the highest literacy rates in the world, considering that Finnish children are not formally taught to read until the age of seven. Before this, focus is on playing and fostering a love of learning. But this is perhaps why Finns love to read so much. A love of reading is instilled from a young age. Approximately twenty million books are sold each year, which averages to about four books per person, including children. Three out of four Finns buy at least one book per year.

But the Finns also make good use of borrowing books for free using an extensive network of libraries. The country has more than 300 central libraries and 500 branch libraries. Then, there are the 150 mobile libraries—buses and boats that are outfitted with shelves that contain, on average, more than 4,000 books, magazines, and newspapers. Books borrowed through mobile libraries account for approximately 10 percent of all book loans in Finland. About 40 percent of all Finnish citizens are active library users. The average Finn visits the library twice per month.

SOCIAL SECURITY

Finns are proud of their social security system, one of the best systems in the world, which provides high-quality living conditions for all. Included in this so-called social security net is social insurance, including pensions, disability and unemployment benefits, and workers' compensation; welfare, which provides services for families, the elderly, and the disabled; and a comprehensive health care system. To provide the capital for this system, Finnish workers pay higher tax rates than workers in other countries. The average income tax, including insurance fees, is approximately 30 percent of an average worker's earnings.

PUBLIC HEALTH CARE

A generous public health care plan is available for all Finnish residents, although Finns may also choose to purchase private health care if they prefer. Health care is not entirely free, although it is heavily subsidized. Patients may pay up to approximately 60 euros per year for one treatment. Small fees are charged for doctor visits, X-rays, screenings and vaccinations, emergency hospital treatment, and home care services. Finns are also expected to pay part of the cost of prescribed medicines; costs for medicine can not exceed approximately 600 euros per year per person.

Workers in Finland receive an allowance of up to 80 percent of their salary for each day that they are ill, and for those out of a job, a minimum daily allowance is also given. The cost of private medical care is also partially reimbursed. War veterans and those born in 1956 and after are entitled to free dental treatment.

A WELFARE STATE

Finland provides a tax-free child allowance to each family per child until the child reaches the age of seventeen. This allowance amounts to approximately 100 euros per month per child and increases based on the amount of children in a family. Families with children under the age of three receive

The population of Finland is aging rapidly, with the government providing ample services for its elderly citizens.

an additional child homecare allowance. Single parents and parents of children with disabilities receive additional financial assistance.

Trade unions operate voluntary unemployment benefit funds, which members can draw from if they are laid off work. The funds are provided by the state and employers and from contributions of the members themselves.

There is a maximum annual amount that can be paid as an unemployment allowance for a period of three years. Workers not covered by union funds are paid an unemployment allowance by the state to meet basic needs.

In Finland, even those who have never worked receive a national pension once they reach the retirement age of sixty-five. This applies to both men and women. In some occupations, the retirement age may be lower. The national pension is based on the wealth and income of each individual. For those who have worked before retiring, an employment pension linked to their previous earnings and number of years worked is also payable. The employment pension is paid only after forty years of work. The earnings-related pension used to be capped at a maximum of 60 percent of the last-drawn salary but this limit was eliminated in 2005 as it discouraged people from working once they had reached this maximum. If a person receives a large employment pension, his or her national pension will be smaller.

CARE FOR THE ELDERLY

As the elderly make up a large percentage of the Finnish population—and this percentage is increasing each year—the Finnish government offers services to enable the elderly to live well as long as possible.

The elderly in Finland prefer to be independent of their families, living in apartment blocks built specially for them so that they can socialize with people of their own age. Municipalities also extend some help by arranging services such as cleaning, shopping, and cooking for a token fee. They also organize senior citizen centers for the elderly to meet and obtain information. For those too old to look after themselves, there are senior citizens' homes.

The Finns prefer to have their elderly spend their last days in a hospital that can try to make their stay as comfortable and painfree as possible. As with marriage, the majority of Finns prefer to have a Christian burial even if they had never been active church members.

INTERNET LINKS

http://www.smithsonianmag.com/ist/?next=/innovation/why-are-finlands-schools-successful-49859555
This *Smithsonian* article delves into why the Finnish educational system has produced some of the world's best-educated people.

www.timeforkids.com/destination/finland/day-in-life
Follow a typical eleven-year-old Finnish student around for the day.

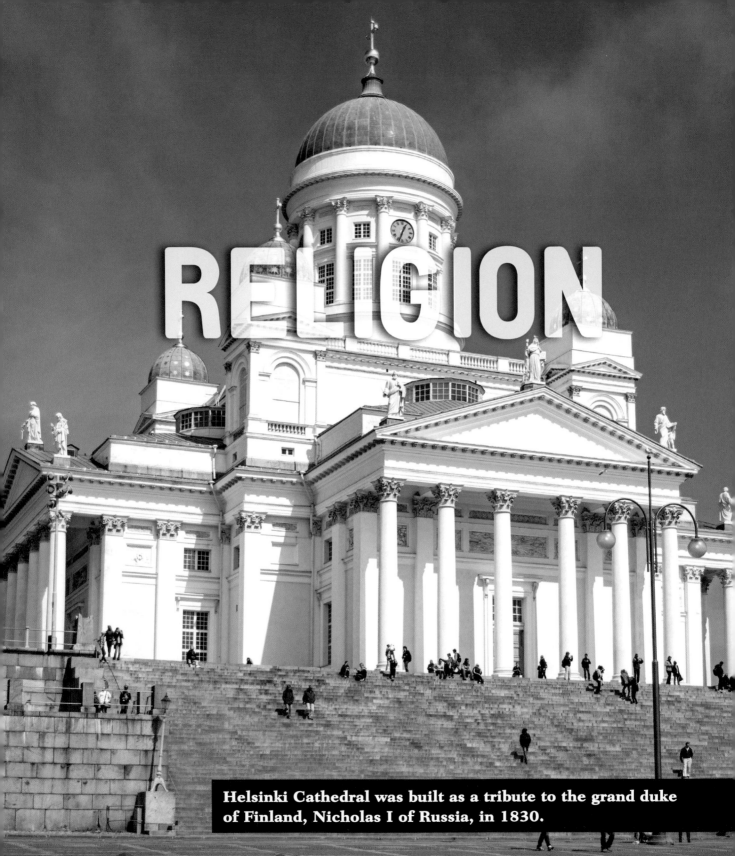

RELIGION

Helsinki Cathedral was built as a tribute to the grand duke of Finland, Nicholas I of Russia, in 1830.

MOST FINNS IDENTIFY WITH THE Christian religion. They follow one of two state churches: the Evangelical Lutheran Church or the Orthodox Church. The Evangelical Lutheran Church of Finland is the primary religious body, and approximately 73 percent of the population identifies as members of this church. Less than 5 percent of the population belongs to other Christian denominations, and other practiced faiths in Finland include Islam and Judaism. Increasingly, Finns attend religious services only for special occasions. The average Finn attends church twice a year.

The Orthodox Church largely gained power in Sweden through its historical ties with Russia and, thus, evolved from the Byzantine Orthodox Church. The Roman Catholic Church grew its influence in Finland from ties in Sweden, where Roman Catholicism was influential.

8

Today's most rapidly growing religion in Finland is Islam. As the number of immigrants in Finland increased during the late twentieth and early twenty-first centuries, many residents of Finland from Arab countries brought their religion with them. Today, there are dozens of mosques and Islamic societies and about fifty thousand practicing Muslims living in Finland.

THE ROMAN CATHOLIC CHURCH

Before approximately 1000 CE, Finnish paganism was the primary religion of the area. Christianity began to gain converts in the country in the eleventh century, with the arrival of missionaries from other parts of Europe, including Anglo-Saxon England. St. Henry, the patron saint of Finland, arrived in 1155 CE, marking the official beginning of Roman Catholicism in the country.

Ulrika Eleonora Church in Kristinestad showcases traditional Finnish architecture.

The Roman Catholic Church used ritual, pomp, and pageantry in ceremonies to convert the nature-worshipping Finns. Masses were conducted mostly in Latin except for the Lord's Prayer, the Creed, and salutations to the Virgin Mary, which were said in Finnish. Incense, holy water, and other religious items were used for all ceremonies.

The first Finnish churches were built from logs. But when Catholicism took root, these churches were replaced by rough-hewn stone churches that were decorated with brick gables and shingle-covered, steeply pitched roofs. These churches soon became an integral part of the landscape in southwest Finland and the Åland Islands. In the thirteenth century, Finland's only cathedral was built in Turku, which became the seat of the bishop.

In the seventeenth century the basilica type of architecture was replaced by a cruciform ground plan (shaped like a cross), with the altar and pulpit situated near the intersection to allow the congregation a better view of church proceedings.

THE PROTESTANT REFORMATION

The Protestant Reformation, begun by Martin Luther in Germany in 1517, spread to Finland in the 1520s. This was a movement that challenged the authority of the Catholic Church and led to various reforms. As opposed

BRINGING THE PROTESTANT REFORMATION HOME

One man is credited with bringing Lutheranism back to Finland. Sent to study in Wittenberg, Germany, in 1536 by the bishop of Turku, Mikael Agricola studied under Protestant reformer Martin Luther. Famously, Martin Luther had critiqued the Catholic Church by sending his Ninety-Five Theses *to the archbishop of Mainz in 1517.*

Returning back home to Turku in 1539, Agricola began his position as rector of the Turku School. Spreading news of Lutheranism and his critiques of the Catholic Church, Agricola taught many students. He was elected bishop of Turku in 1554 and became the first Lutheran bishop in Finland. Due to this one man's efforts, Lutheranism became the main religion in Finland early on in the history of Protestantism.

A sculptor's depiction of Mikael Agricola

to the official reforms that were instituted in Norway despite widespread opposition, Finland was gently converted to Lutheranism. Finnish Lutherans gradually instituted reforms while safeguarding Finnish traditions. The Lutheran Church was not fully established in Finland until 1598, when the final Roman Catholic king abdicated his throne.

The use of Latin in church services was replaced by Swedish, which was first used in 1531 in Turku Cathedral. By the end of the 1530s bilingual services in Swedish and Finnish were the norm in churches. In general, there was no opposition to the changes brought about by the Reformation. Many did not understand the significance of the reforms, though some did initially miss the ceremonial aspects associated with the Catholic liturgy.

The educational ties with southern Europe's old universities and cultural centers ended with the Reformation. Finns were now sent to study in places such as Wittenberg and Rostock in Germany and Prague in what is now the Czech Republic. In 1642, a Bible in Finnish was finally produced.

THE CATHOLIC COUNTER-REFORMATION

John III of Sweden

A brief resurgence of Catholicism, called the Counter-Reformation, began in 1568. Under the reign of Swedish king John III, Jesuits began to gain dominance in Stockholm Theological University. John III also encouraged the readoption of several Catholic tenants. He drew up a plan to blend the two religions together in the Swedish Empire and submitted it to the pope for his approval. However, the pope rejected John III's plan because he perceived some of his suggestions, such as allowing priests to marry, to be too controversial. There was also opposition to John III's religious policy in Sweden and Finland, especially when he came up with the *Red Book*, which outlined more Catholic forms of worship to be adopted in churches.

The Counter-Reformation movement did not gain much headway, and the Protestant Church became firmly established in the latter part of the sixteenth and early seventeenth centuries. Legislation was passed prohibiting citizens from holding onto variants of the Catholic and Protestant faiths, such as sacramentalist, Zwinglist, Calvinist, Anabaptist, or any other heretical doctrines. In 1617, the state went further by issuing a law that forbade conversion to Catholicism. Those who did so risked being banned from the country.

FINLAND'S ORTHODOX CHURCH

Twelfth-century missionaries from the east of Finland in Russia brought the Orthodox Church as far west as central Finland in Tavastia. However, the religion was largely confined to areas east of the country. Religious extremism in the seventeenth century led to the persecution of the Orthodox community in Finland. Many Finnish Orthodox Christians fled to Russia due to this oppression, which further cemented the secondary position of the

religion in the country. When Finland became an autonomous grand duchy of Russia from 1808 to 1917, however, the presence of the Orthodox Church became more pronounced. There was an Orthodox church or chapel wherever a Russian garrison was stationed.

Today, the Orthodox Church continues to thrive. It is the second-largest church in Finland with a membership of about sixty thousand.

Uspenski Cathedral is part of the Eastern Orthodox Church in Helsinki.

THE ROLE OF CHRISTIANITY

Today, approximately 4.1 million Finns are members of the Lutheran Church of Finland, making it the third-largest Lutheran congregation in the world. There are approximately 408 independent parishes in the country, grouped together under nine dioceses, each of which has its own bishop. However, a decline in churchgoers has led many Finnish parishes to combine in recent years. Following perceived homophobic remarks made by religious officials, many Finns decided to leave the church. While Lutheran traditions still

EI
30

TYHJÄÄ
0

POI

TURUN KRISTILLINEN
OPISTO

In 2010, the Synod voted to permit pastors to give blessings to same-sex couples.

dominate Finnish society, including getting married in church and having children baptized and confirmed, organized religious affiliation is declining rapidly in Finland. Today, approximately 22 percent of Finns consider themselves atheists.

THE SYNOD

The separation of church and state occurred in Finland in 1869, with the passage of the Church Act. This act also provided for the creation of the Synod, which is the church's own legislative body. The Synod has the sole right to make changes to the Church Act, although these changes must be approved by the Finnish parliament. The Synod also looks after the operations of the churches and their finances. Since 2010, the Synod has become more liberal in terms of LGBT issues, taking a stance in favor of same-sex marriage.

The ordination of women priests—after a controversial debate—was consented to by the Synod in 1986. Parliament approved the amendment to the Church Act in 1988, the year when the first graduating class of female theological students was ordained. The office of bishop is also open to women.

SEPARATION OF CHURCH AND STATE

Although the church and the state of Finland are independent, the church still has the right to levy taxes on its membership. The church tax for all members of the Lutheran Church of Finland and the Finnish Orthodox Church is, on average, 1.4 percent. It is collected by the Finnish internal revenue department on behalf of the church. This income provides nearly all of the services provided by Finland's two state churches, including keeping birth and death registers and maintaining cemeteries.

Finland granted its citizens complete freedom of religion in 1923. Depending on their beliefs, parents may have their children study religion at school or not.

The third most important church in Finland is the Pentecostal movement with a congregation of fifty thousand. The other churches are much smaller in membership and include Jehovah's Witnesses, Seventh-Day Adventists, the Finnish Free Church, and the Roman Catholic Church.

INTERNET LINKS

http://evl.fi/EVLen.nsf/
This is the official site of Finland's national church.

www.uskonnot.fi/English
This site is part of an academic project to study religions in Finland and offers a wealth of valuable information on the topic.

LANGUAGE

Suomi-Finland

80

Käytä aina ajovaloja
Geavat álo vuodjinčuovggaid
Bruk alltid nærlys
Always use headlights

LAPPI
SÁPMI

UTSJOKI
OHCEJOHKA

At the border of Norway and Finland, signs are written in English, Finnish, and the Sami language.

9

FINLAND IS MULTILINGUAL. THE country has two main official languages—Finnish and Swedish—as well as official minority languages, including Sami, Romani, and Karelian. Finnish is spoken by about 92 percent of the population as their native language, while Swedish is spoken as a mother tongue by approximately 5 percent of the population, although it is the second language of 44 percent of Finns. In addition, 70 percent of Finns speak English, and many also speak Russian or Estonian. Sami languages were granted official status in 1991 and claim over 1,800 native speakers today, mostly living in Lapland.

Today, only 5.4 million people speak Finnish. Since very few foreigners know the language, many Finns have had to become proficient in other languages, usually English, German, or Russian. Finnish is an interesting language because it is not Indo-European in origin, which means that it does not share a common ancestor with other European languages. Rather, Finnish is a Uralic language, which includes Estonian and other languages spoken in the Baltic region. There are approximately

Before the nineteenth century, Finnish poetry and folktales reflected a strong Swedish influence. The Finns' pride in their own language and culture began to take root only in the latter half of the nineteenth century, thanks to the efforts of scholars like Elias Lönnrot, creator of the *Kalevala* and one of the first university professors of Finnish, and J. V. Snellman.

twenty-five million people who speak one of the thirty-eight languages in the Uralic family. Hungarian is also a Uralic language, although it differs greatly from Finnish. Sami languages are also Uralic in origin, although they are distinct enough not to be easily understood by Finns.

Finnish has borrowed many words—approximately 15 percent—from other languages, particularly from Swedish, Russian, and English. Many new technological terms are adopted from English into Finnish.

Finnish is written with the Swedish version of the Latin alphabet. This means that, instead of five vowels, it has eight: *a*, *e*, *i*, *o*, *u*, *y*, *ä*, and *ö*. In addition to ä and ö, Finnish also has the additional letter *Å*.

DISTINCTIVE SOUNDS

The pronunciation of Finnish words is very different from English, however it is also very regular. Once you understand the rules governing Finnish pronunciation, it is easy to know how words should be pronounced. However, sounding like a native speaker is still difficult due to the language's distinctive sounds.

Finnish vowels are pronounced the same way as in English except for the following:

- *y* is pronounced like the German ü with the umlaut.
- *ä* is like the *a* in *fact*.
- *ö* is pronounced like the second *e* in *theater*.

If a vowel occurs twice, as in *aa* or *ii*, there is a slight drag in the pronunciation, such as in *aah* or *ee*.

Certain consonants are also pronounced differently from those in English:

- *z* is pronounced as *ts* and can be written as such.
- *v* and *w* are considered the same letter.
- *h* has a weak sound except at the end of a closed syllable, when it is pronounced with more force, as in the German *ch* in *ich*.
- *j* is pronounced like *y* in *yellow*.
- *r* is rolled.

Double consonants, such as *kk* in *Keskiviikko* (KES-kee-VEEK-oh), which means "Wednesday," or *aa* in *saari* (SAAH-ri), meaning "island," are held longer. *Ng* and *nk* are two syllables and are pronounced as *ng-ng* and *ng-k*. For instance, *vangit*, which means "prisons," is pronounced "VAHNG-ngit." The syllable *np* is pronounced as *mp*; so *olenpa*, meaning "I am," becomes "OH-lem-pa."

The Finnish language does not use articles of speech such as *a* or *the*. Prepositions are rare, and the language does not distinguish between male and female pronouns—both are referred to as *hän* (hahn), or "hand." As in French, Spanish, and other European languages, the Finns have two different ways of saying "you": the informal *sinä* (see-NA) when addressing close friends and relatives and the formal *Te* (tay) when speaking to acquaintances or at a professional level.

FINNISH FORMS OF ADDRESS

Finnish forms of address began to take root in the eighteenth century, following the influence of other languages and cultures in the country. In Finland, it is not common to use forms of address based solely on one's gender or marital status, such as "Mr.," "Mrs.," or "Ms." Instead, Finns address people depending on their status and profession. For example, if you want to address a man with the last name of Rotko, who is the managing director of a bank, you would say address him as *Maisteri* (MAIS-ter-ri) Rotko. This means "bank director Rotko."

A LOGICAL LANGUAGE

Finnish is a very logical language, although many English speakers find it difficult to learn because it is very different from other European languages. It sounds melodical, as it depends on different intonations and vowels. Consonants are very uncommon, and Finnish words cannot start with two consonants at once. However, diphthongs, or two different vowels grouped together, occur frequently.

Words in Finnish can have many different forms (called grammatical cases)—as many as fifteen in some cases. In contrast, Latin words have only six different forms. The form of a Finnish word depends on the context. For example, *talo* (TAH-lo) means "house." To say "in the house," the word changes to *talossa* (TA-lo-sa), and to mean "of the house," it becomes *talon* (TA-lon).

For a time, Finnish as a language was threatened when, during periods of foreign occupation, languages such as Swedish and Russian were used instead. Despite much pressure, the patriotic Finns stuck to their own language. Like many other languages, however, new Finnish words have evolved over time to reflect outside influences, especially English. Thus, there is *rokkimusiikki* (ROK-kee-MOO-see-kee) for "rock music" and *bandi* (BAHN-dee) for "band." While some Finnish words are a bit of a tongue twister, there are others a person is able to pronounce easily and even recognize their meanings right away:

- *hotelli* (HO-tel-li) . . . . hotel
- *motelli* (MO-tel-li) . . . motel
- *auto* (AW-toh) . . . . . car
- *taksi* (TAK-si) . . . . taxi
- *dieseli* (DEEY-sel-li) . . . diesel

To say "yes" in Finnish, one says *kyllä* (KOO-la). The word "no" is *ei* (ay), while "thank you" is *kiitos* (KEEH-tos). For "please," one says *olkaa hyvä* (OHL-kaah HOO-vah), and "good-bye" is *näkemiin* (NA-kem-een).

THE FATHER OF WRITTEN FINNISH

The Finnish written language was created by one man, Mikael Agricola (1510—1557), who is remembered as the "father of literary Finnish." Before Agricola, the literary language in Finland, as in the rest of Europe, was Latin. As the bishop of Turku, Agricola began to reform the Finnish church during the Lutheran Reformation. Part of this task was translating religious writings, and especially the Bible, from Latin to Finnish so that the common people— those who did not have Latin training—could have access to the religion. His translations set the spelling rules for Finnish that are still in use today.

It was Agricola who translated the New Testament in 1548 and the Psalms of David in 1551. He was among the first batch of students at the new University of Wittenberg to study under German Protestant reformers Martin Luther and Philipp Melanchthon after the Reformation found its way to Europe. After three years, he returned to Finland, where he was appointed a schoolmaster in Turku, then a member of the cathedral chapter, before becoming a bishop in 1554.

TOVE JANSSON: CREATOR OF THE MOOMINS

One of Finland's best-known writers is Tove Jansson (1914–2001). Her books about "little trolls" and their adventures in Moominland are favorites among children in Scandinavia and have even gained a following in Japan. Although Jansson's stories are for children, they often address grown-up themes, like the Cold War or facing a midlife crisis. She was awarded the Hans Christian Andersen Award in 1966 for her contributions to children's literature. Jansson, whose father was a sculptor and mother an illustrator, was also an accomplished painter. A member of the Finnish-Swedish minority, her books were originally written in Swedish and have been translated into thirty-three languages. They are the most-translated works of Finnish literature after the Kalevala *and books by Mika Waltari. A theme park devoted to the Moomins exists outside Naantali, near Turku.*

His first work in the Finnish language was the Finnish ABC book *ABC-kiriai* in 1543, followed by the Book of Prayer from the Bible that same year. The Finns are truly indebted to him, for it was Agricola who created the written Finnish language, coining many new words that are still in use today. Thanks to his pioneering efforts, the complete Bible was finally translated in 1642, an enormous task that took nearly a century.

INTERNET LINKS

ielanguages.com/finnish.html
This site offers free lessons to learn Finnish.

tovejansson.com
The official site of Finland's most famous author.

ARTS

This 1881 illustration depicts a scene from the *Kalevala*.

10

THE OLDEST FINNISH LITERATURE was written down in the eighteenth and nineteenth centuries after being passed down orally for many generations and consists of folk poetry, songs, proverbs, and legends. This includes the Finnish national epic, the *Kalevala*, which includes stories that most likely date back thousands of years prior to its publication in 1835. Fredrik Pacius composed the Finnish national anthem, "Our Land," based on the great nationalist epic poem *The Tales of Ensign Stål*, written by Johan Ludvig Runeberg, the national poet of Finland, in 1848.

"Not so long ago, in the tiny, isolated villages of Finland, where prolonged summer days gave way to endless winter nights, people would pass the time by singing the many adventures of their favorite heroes: the mighty, magical men and women of ancient days."
—From the *Kalevala*, as retold by Aaron Shepard

EARLY ART FORMS

The earliest text in an early Finnish language was discovered in 1957 during a Soviet expedition in Novgorod. Written on a piece of birchbark, the short text invokes the Estonian god of the sky. Before the codification of the Finnish language by Mikael Agricola in the sixteenth century, most literature was remembered and spread orally. Runes were folk poems that were sung in order to better memorize their contents. Rune singing would be passed from generation to generation in a family, and singers would be accompanied by the harp-like *kantele* (KAHN-tay-leh), an ancient Finnish instrument.

Rune singers were primarily women, although men tended to sing epic poems, and women the lyrical ones. In the nineteenth century, many of the rune singers were old and some were blind, like the well-known Miihkali Perttunen, the son of Finland's greatest rune singer, Arhippa Perttunen, who contributed one-third of the material for *Old Kalevala*.

THE MODERN PERIOD

Johan Ludvig Runeberg (1804—1877) is Finland's national poet, although he was born into a Swedish-speaking family and wrote primarily in Swedish. Born on the coast, Runeberg spent much of his life in the rural backwoods of central Finland, working as a tutor for a wealthy family at their country estate. Here, Runeberg observed the lives of rural peasants. Inspired by their strength, he romanticized their hard lives in his earliest poems.

The Elk Hunters, written in 1832, rose to the status of a national epic. It was among the first works to be translated into Finnish by the newly launched Finnish Literature Society. But it was Runeberg's *Vänrikki Stoolin Tarinat* (*The Tales of Ensign Stål*) that catapulted him to fame as a national poet. The ballad series was about Finland's war of 1808—1809 and the bravery of the Finnish soldiers fighting alongside Swedish troops. The first of these ballads was "Our Land," which was later adopted as Finland's national anthem, with music by Pacius.

Aleksis Kivi (1834—1872) wrote the first novel in Finnish, entitled *Seven Brothers*. The stubbornness, endurance, and love of liberty of the brothers in the story continue to elicit the admiration of Finns today. Minna Canth (1844—1897) was Finland's first major playwright. Her works, drawing on her experience as a wife and widow, were an inspiration to the workers' and women's movements. The best-known novel in Finland is *The Unknown Soldier* by Väinö Linna. A powerful antiwar statement, it is a realistic portrayal of war from the point of view of an ordinary soldier.

THE *KALEVALA* AND ELIAS LÖNNROT

The Kalevala *is recognized as Finland's national epic poem. It was compiled from Finnish folklore by Elias Lönnrot (1802–1884), who recorded the folklore from rune singers. The work took several years to finish and represents the first written collection of Finnish folk poetry.*

Lönnrot was born into a poor family in a small village west of Helsinki. He learned to read at home and only started school when he was twelve. He went on to study medicine and become a doctor, but his passion was collecting Finnish folk songs. It was in the early 1830s that he had the idea of compiling a series of miniature epics based on the exploits of heroes, such as Väinämöinen, who were featured in folk poems. His compilation was published in 1833 as the Proto-Kalevala.

In 1834, Lönnrot was granted a scholarship to travel and collect more folklore. The result was Old Kalevala, *published in 1835. As time went on, Lönnrot gathered even more material, and all these were compiled into the second edition* Kalevala, *which appeared in 1849 and has since been considered the foundation of Finnish culture. The "new"* Kalevala *had fifty cantos, a canto being a main division of a long poem. It stimulated interest in Finnish history and later became a symbol in the drive for national independence. The epic has been translated into forty-three languages and is the best-known work of Finnish literature.*

Lönnrot collected much of his material in Karelia, where rune singers can still be found today. His work was a boost to the local arts. It sparked interest in the systematic collection of folk poetry, a task that is now undertaken by the Folklore Archive of the Finnish Literature Society, the biggest of its kind in the world.

> *I have a good mind*
> *take into my head*
> *to start off singing*
> *begin reciting*
> *reeling off a tale of kin*
> *and singing a tale of kind.*
> *The words unfreeze*
> *in my mouth*
> *and the phrases are tumbling*
> *upon my tongue they scramble*
> *along my teeth they scatter.*

—*The opening lines from the* Kalevala, *translated into English by Keith Bosley, 1989*

Finland is known for its composers, its architecture, and its avant garde design. But it is also known for its heavy metal. In fact, the country is so taken with this musical genre that Finns can go to church for a Metal Mass.

Called Metallimessu *in Finnish, the Metal Mass pairs heavy metal music with biblical verses and lyrics. It is combined with aspects of a traditional mass, including a sermon and the Eucharist. The first Metal Mass occurred in 2006 at the Tuska Metal Music Festival in Helsinki. After, a Metal Mass bus famously toured the country, bringing these new Lutheran services to teens across Finland. Many older Finns dislike these new masses. However, it is a way for churches to bring in younger members and a unique way to combine the Finns' love of heavy metal with the country's traditional Lutheranism.*

MUSICAL TRADITIONS

Finnish folk music is typically divided into three categories: Karelian traditional music, mainstream Nordic folk, and Sami music. Of the three, Karelian music is said to most purely express traditional Finnish beliefs. In recent years, folk music has resurged and been integrated into popular music.

Many classical musicians gained fame in Finland. The first notable name in Finnish music was Fredrik Pacius, who composed the score for "Our Land." He also set up the first orchestra and choir in Helsinki. Finnish opera singers have also met with success on the international stage. Soprano Aino Ackté set the pace in the early 1900s. She founded the Savonlinna Opera Festival, which helped to nurture future opera talents. Other famous names in opera include mezzo-soprano Monica Groop, soprano Karita Mattila, and Matti Salminen, whose rich bass voice has been likened to that of the legendary Finnish opera singer Martti Talvela (1935—1989). All of these contemporary opera singers have performed in the world's great opera houses.

The Finns are fond of light music by dance bands and, for many years, Toivo Kärki reigned as the most popular composer and Dallapé as the best dance band. Finland has also made a mark internationally in the world of popular music with hits from groups such as Trio Töykeät (jazz), HIM (rock), Nightwish (metal), and Värttinä (folk), as well as electronic dance DJ Ville Virtanen, better known as Darude.

The Finns take their music seriously as it is considered a way of preserving their cultural heritage. Music is offered as a subject in some schools in Finland, while as many as fifty thousand students take lessons in 150 private music institutes. There are thirty professional orchestras in the country, more per capita than anywhere else in the world.

Many Finnish musicians, composers, and conductors have made a name for themselves, not only at home, but also abroad. Some of them are very young, such as Mikko Franck, who started conducting professionally in 1997, when he was only seventeen. Before turning twenty-three, he made his conducting debut on the international stage, leading orchestras in Berlin, London, Israel, and Munich. In 2004, he was appointed the music director for the Finnish National Opera. Other famous conductors include Esa-Pekka Salonen, Osmo Vänskä, and Jukka-Pekka Saraste.

FINLAND'S MOST FAMOUS COMPOSER

Jean Sibelius is Finland's most famous composer and is well known internationally as one of the greatest composers of his time. Not only is Sibelius recognized for his music, but he is often credited with helping Finland to forge its national identity after the country gained independence from Russia. Indeed, *Finlandia*, Sibelius's most famous piece, became an anthem for the Finnish independence movement. Written in 1899, it depicts important moments in Finnish history, arousing strong feelings of national

"Finland is a famously introverted nation. Finnish joke: How can you tell if a Finn likes you? He's staring at your shoes instead of his own."

—Susan Cain

Jean Sibelius is Finland's most beloved composer.

sentiment among its Finnish audience. For many years, Russia censored this piece due to the nationalist pride it expressed, and the piece would be performed secretively under different names.

Sibelius may have been Finnish, but he was also part of a greater European musical tradition. He traveled to Munich and Bayreuth in Germany in 1894 and was influenced by Tchaikovsky and German symphonic composers like Wagner and Beethoven. His *First Symphony*, first performed in 1899, signaled a moving away from his national heritage. In his later compositions, particularly the *Sixth Symphony* (1923) and *Seventh Symphony* (1924), Sibelius came into his own as a composer, unbridled by time or place, and gained international recognition as a composer. His symphonies, *Finlandia* and a composition called the *Karelia Suite* (1893), are played by orchestras all over the world, creating an awareness of Finland in the international music scene.

DANCE

Folk dances are an important part of Finnish history, although they are today only performed at special events and outdoor festivals. The earliest known folk dances were first performed in the Middle Ages as chain dances even before instrumental accompaniment was adopted. Today, these dances can still be performed at weddings. The modern dance movement in Finland, which began in 1922 with the founding of the Finnish National Ballet, is still going strong.

While Margaretha von Bahr is considered the most respected of Finnish dancers, it is Jorma Uotinen who is credited with revolutionizing Finnish dance. Uotinen is Finland's best-known choreographer, performer, and proponent of experimental dance. During his tenure as artistic director for the Finland National Ballet from 1992 to 2001 he introduced a challenging repertoire that included his dynamic interpretations of classical ballet as well as contemporary dance. He is now the artistic director of the annual Kuopio Dance and Music Festival. Under his guidance, the festival has gained an international reputation, which further enhances the status of Finnish dance.

Although classical dance is highly appreciated by Finnish audiences, there is one form of dance that is much loved in the country—tango. In Finland specially composed tango music has helped keep this dance alive over the years. Today there are many Finnish nightspots offering tango dancing. An annual Tango Festival at Seinäjoki in Southern Ostrobothnia lures thousands of visitors, and a Tango King and Tango Queen are crowned every year.

FILM

The Finnish film industry has a long history, with the first screenings taking place in 1896, only one year after the first public movie screening in the world. The first "talking" movie was produced in Finland in 1931. Today, between fifteen and twenty Finnish films are produced each year. One classic is Edvin Laine's 1955 film *Tuntematon Sotilas* (*The Unknown Soldier*), which was adapted from Väinö Linna's popular novel of the same name about the war between Finland and the Soviet Union that lasted from 1941 to 1944.

Beginning in the 1980s, Aki and Mika Kaurismäki led a wave of revival in the Finnish film industry. Mika Kaurismäki's films often have a touch of black humor. Among his films are *The Clan* (1980), a crime story; *Cha Cha Cha* (1989), a comedy; and *Amazon* (1990), an adventure film. Mika now spends more time making films in the United States, such as *L.A. Without a Map* (1998). Aki Kaurismäki, his younger brother, has built up a following as a cult director. Noted for his working-class trilogy, *Shadows in Paradise* (1986), *Ariel* (1988), and *The Match Factory Girl* (1990), he has also gone international, directing films in Paris, such as *Leningrad Cowboys Go America* (1989) and *La Vie Bohème* (1992). Aki Kaurismäki put Finnish filmmaking on the map when his film *The Man Without a Past* won the Grand Prix du Jury at the Cannes Film Festival in 2002. The movie was also nominated for an Academy Award in the Best Foreign Language Film category in 2003. In 2015, the internationally produced drama *Return* was selected as Finland's entry for Best Foreign Language Film for the Academy Awards. It was selected for the short list but was not nominated. The film, directed by legendary Finnish director Klaus Härö, was also nominated for a Golden Globe. In total, four of Härö's films have been selected as entries for the Academy Awards.

THEATRICAL ARTS

Theater began during ancient times in Finland as a way of performing folk rituals associated with hunting and fishing. However, these pagan performances died out with the arrival of Christianity in the twelfth century. From then on, Christians began their own theatrical performances.

Although the earliest drama performance in Finland was held in Turku in the 1650s, it was not until the nineteenth century that the country's first theaters were built. The first Finnish play, *Silmänkääntäjät* (*The Conjurers*) by Pietari Hannikainen, was performed in 1847, but it was only in 1869, when Aleksis Kivi's *Lea* was staged, that Finnish-language theater really took off. Finland has around sixty professional theatrical troupes and many amateur and youth groups. The main theatrical cities are Helsinki, Turku, and Tampere, although there are cultural institutes in many other areas. Theater enjoys adequate state funding as it is seen as an important part of national culture.

The support of the media in publicizing theater activities, the existence of numerous festivals as a platform for showcasing theater, and an inherent love for the theater among Finns have all contributed to its healthy growth.

ARCHITECTURE

Finland's architecture reflects the country's varied cultural heritage. Older buildings located in urban areas in Finland typically reflect Swedish and Russian influences. Early Finnish architecture relied on wood constructions, particularly the *kota*, a wooden structure covered with fabric or moss. During the Middle Ages, stone castles and wooden churches with detailed engravings were built all over the country. Unfortunately, many of these earlier wooden structures were destroyed by fire.

At the beginning of the nineteenth century, the Romantic architectural style was a blend of Karelian wooden architecture, medieval stonework, and art nouveau style. The 1920s saw the development of a more restrained interpretation of classical architecture, followed by more functional designs as characterized by the works of Alvar Aalto (1898–1976), the father of modern Finnish architecture. Aalto has been influential in regional and urban planning, and the design of homes, churches, and larger buildings, as well as interior decoration and industrial art. His last important work was Finlandia Hall in Helsinki, a monumental concert and conference center in white marble. He considered the forest to be

This house was built in traditional Karelian fashion.

Finland's most important resource and continually created links back to the forest. Aalto's wife, Aino Marsio Aalto (1898–1949), is seen today as an important contributor to Aalto's work. She served as his social conscience and followed through after Aalto made the initial sketches.

A particularly well-known Finnish architect is Eliel Saarinen (1873–1950). He designed the Chicago Tribune Building, which set the standard for early skyscrapers in the United States. His son Eero Saarinen (1909–1961) is known for his design of the TWA terminal at John F. Kennedy International Airport in New York City. The terminal looks like a giant prehistoric bird poised to take off in flight.

Raili Pietilä (1923–1993) worked with her husband, Raimo Pietilä (1923–1998), on many projects, including churches, town centers, and the presidential residence. Their design style has been described by many as unconventional.

A high point of Finnish architecture can be seen in the new town of Tapiola. Created in the late 1950s, Tapiola brought together the talents of the most important Finnish architects and urbanists of the time, including Alvar Aalto, Aarne Ervi, Pauli Blomstedt, and Raili and Raimo Pietilä.

Today, the emphasis of Finnish architecture lies in creating a more human touch and harmony with the environment. The restoration and conservation of old buildings are areas of particular interest.

VISUAL ARTS

Early Stone Age carvings are the earliest form of Finnish art and can be found all around Finland. In particular, the first known sculpture discovered in Finland, called the Elk's Head of Huittinen and carved out of soapstone, was dated to approximately 7500 BCE. It is currently in permanent exhibition at the National Museum of Finland in Helsinki.

Finnish art as we know it today began with the founding of the Fine Arts Society of Finland in 1848. The greatest strides were made in the 1890s when interest in the *Kalevala* and Finnish folk poetry was revived. Many artists turned to nature and Karelia as the origin of their cultural past. This gave rise to a movement known as Karelianism, which had themes centered around landscapes and fauna. It led to the flourishing of a period that was acknowledged as the golden age of Finnish art, around the end of the nineteenth century. The famous names of this era include history painter Albert Edelfelt, Akseli

The sculptor Wäinö Aaltonen's depiction of runner Paavo Nurmi

Gallen-Kallela, Eero Järnefelt, Pekka Halonen, and Juha Rissanen.

In sculpture, Wäinö Aaltonen's portrayal of Paavo Nurmi, the Olympic runner, is internationally known. Eila Hiltunen created the Sibelius Monument, which recalls the shape of organ pipes. Located in Helsinki, it is the first completely abstract monument dedicated to a person. In response to criticism, Hiltunen later added a representation of the composer's face.

FINNISH MODERNISM

The Finns are well known for their love of design, and Helsinki was named the World Design Capital in 2012. Many famous Finnish designers are said to have derived inspiration from the natural landscape of Finland and have encapsulated that inspiration into a particular blend of Finnish modernism.

Finnish textiles and rugs reflect the colors of changing seasons, while glass designers adopt many motifs from flora and fauna. Wood remains the most popular material for designers working by hand.

Finnish design was taught as early as the nineteenth century and made its international launch at the Paris World Exhibition in 1900. It has a classic quality about it. Its clean, modern lines have an element of timelessness. The designs are also practical, as reflected in Marimekko's popular textiles for household use, the enamel kitchenware of Heikki Orvola, and the household articles of Timo Sarpaneva. Tapio Wirkkala, a glass designer known for his iceberg designs; Kaj Franck, known for his textures, ceramics, and glass; and Timo Sarpaneva, known for his graphic design and also ceramics and glass creations, have all acquired international reputations.

The artistic designs found in glass and silver objects are good buys for tourists hunting for Finnish products to take home as souvenirs. Equally avant garde in design and style are jewelry and furniture. Many Finnish designers also create designs for industry, and the lines between art and design are constantly being blurred.

INTERNET LINKS

www.britannica.com/topic/Kalevala
Learn more about the history of Finland's national epic.

finland.fi/category/arts-culture
The country's official website offers information about Finnish art and cultural events.

"Art and design in Finland, I realise, are as integral to national identity as salted fish and the Moomins— something that has been recognised by the International Council of Societies of Industrial Design, which has named Helsinki World Design Capital for 2012. This is a country where architect and designer Alvar Aalto is afforded a status akin to that of Shakespeare in England and where, until recently, the government presented all newlyweds with crockery sets made by renowned ceramics producer Arabia.
—journalist Rufus Purdy

LEISURE

Skiing is a beloved pastime in Finland.

11

T'S NOT SURPRISING THAT THE FINNS love the outdoors. Despite often frigid temperatures, the country offers vast swaths of open space where Finns can walk, hike, cycle, and swim. Under "everyman's right," everyone has the right to access nature, and hiking and camping are allowed almost everywhere in Finland. Outdoor sports provide the beautiful backdrop for Finns as they struggle to beat their competitors'—or their own—best time.

The Finns' love of leisure and sport developed over hundreds of years. From the early seventeenth century, the Royal Academy of Turku employed a swordsmanship instructor. Sports were incorporated into military life early on in Finland's history to increase the endurance and physical strength of those in the military. Even today, Finland's army trains its soldiers in long-distance cross-country skiing to develop their endurance.

A love of sports is drilled into civilians, too, from an early age. Young children learn to ski almost as early as they can walk—and these same children continue practicing their sport as long as they can, even into old age. Cross-country skiing is arguably Finland's most popular sport; the 47-mile (75 km) Finlandia Skiing Marathon—which takes skiers from Hämeenlinna to Lahti—is the sport's biggest event. Beginning in 1974 with less than 1,500 participants, today the marathon hosts well over

10,000 skiers each year. It's true: a love of cross-country skiing seems to be in Finnish blood. Even when the snow season is over, you can see Finns wearing short wooden skis fitted with wheels as they "ski" along their neighborhood roads. This is a way for them to train for the upcoming ski season—just after the last season has passed.

But cross-country skiing is not the only beloved sport in Finland. Ice hockey is another of the most popular sports in Finland, and the country has won the world championship twice, in 1995 and 2011. Soccer, called football, is popular here, as it is throughout Europe. (American football also garners a strong following in Finland.) Swimming, too, holds a special place in Finns' hearts and can be practiced year-round—both in heated indoor swimming pools and in the sport of ice swimming, in which holes are cut through thick layers of ice and swimmers dive right in.

While ice hockey is the country's most watched sport, *pesäpallo* (PAY-sa-PAHL-lo) is its national sport. First developed in the 1920s, pesäpallo is a faster version of baseball where the ball is pitched vertically instead of horizontally. The pesäpallo World Cup is played every three years, the last being held in Switzerland in 2015. Another traditional Finnish sport is harness racing, which is the most attended sporting event in Finland following ice hockey. In recent years, Formula One racing has also gained popularity among Finnish viewers.

HIKING AND EVERYMAN'S RIGHT

As Finland is one of the least densely populated countries in Europe, there are ample opportunities to hike across untouched natural landscapes. In some areas, hikers can journey for hours, if not days, without meeting another person. In the south, forests are owned by locals who cultivate the trees for timber, although "everyman's right" stipulates that hikers can crisscross these areas as well, whether or not they are privately owned.

A network of well-marked trails and closely spaced footpaths makes hiking easy, even for someone unfamiliar with the Finnish forest. The Finns have a choice of twenty-nine nature reserves to hike in. These have wilderness huts and camping facilities for overnight hikers. Often, Finnish families enjoy spending the day in the forest for easy hikes, where children can gather mushrooms and pick wild berries.

ORIENTEERING

Orienteering is not just one sport, but a family of sports, grouped together by the requirement that competitors, normally using a compass and map, make use of their navigational skills. Orienteering is popular in Finland due to Finland's wide-open spaces and naturally rugged terrain. Begun as a training exercise in the military, orienteering competitions involve an orienteer who must race against the clock to complete a route before his or her competitors. Finland currently ranks third in the world in the sport, and there are plenty of orienteering clubs across the country in which Finns can participate.

A Finnish name that is synonymous with orienteering worldwide is Suunto, maker of compasses and precision instruments. Today, Suunto also produces much of the equipment used for orienteering, including control flags and course markers.

Exploring nature is considered a basic human right in Finland.

WATER SPORTS

Water sports are big business in Finland, considering that 10 percent of the country is made up of water and it has a 25,000-mile (40,000 km) coastline. Off the coast sit thirty thousand islands, where boating enthusiasts can discover the country's unique beauty. During the boating season, which lasts from late May to late September, boat sails dot the horizon across the open sea. Canoeists and kayakers can take to one of Finland's 188,000 lakes, exploring each unique shoreline. The waters of the Baltic can be tricky, with rocks and reefs extending just below the surface, and few gusts of wind. But this is a fun challenge for Finland's adventurous sailors, who enjoy exploring the skerries and channels between the islands of the archipelagos.

The Finns enjoy angling for fish when they are picnicking by a stream or lake and will pan-fry their catch in the open air. Anglers can also fish from boats out at sea or from the coastline. The species of fish caught are usually perch, cod, pike, whitefish, rainbow trout, sea trout, and Atlantic salmon. Even in winter, when the lakes freeze, the Finns fish simply by making holes in the ice!

HUNTING

About 6 percent of Finland's population, around three hundred thousand people, hold hunting permits, which allow them to hunt across Finland's plains and forests. This is the largest percentage of hunters by country in Europe. Hunting is a popular pastime in Finland, where there are over forty thousand hunting clubs. But it is also highly regulated. To hunt in Finland, one has to have not only hunting rights, but also a firearms license and a Finnish hunting card. In certain circumstances, for example to hunt deer or bears, hunters must also pass a shooting test and hold species-specific hunting permits.

The hunting season starts at the end of August. The participants are usually men, and a strong sense of camaraderie develops as they share the tasks of camping, picnicking, and stalking prey in the woods or out on lakes in boats, or with a dog if they are hunting birds. Hunting has also become a big earner for tourism, especially in the north. Every year, sportsmen from central Europe travel to Finland to partake in the unique wilderness experience found in the vast wild landscape of Lapland.

HARNESS RACING

Harness racing is a particularly Finnish sport, and a popular one among Finns. Developed hundreds of years ago with the practice of racing back home from church in rural areas of Finland, harness racing is the second-most attended sport in the country. Also called trotting, harness racing in Finland involves specially bred cold-blood Finnhorses, that trot while pulling two-wheeled carts. Jockeys sit aboard the carts and guide the horse, sometimes using a light whip.

There are forty-three racetracks in Finland, which hold about seven hundred races annually. The biggest racetrack in Finland is Vermo, located on the outskirts of Helsinki.

WHITE-WATER RAFTING

White-water rafting, also called "shooting the rapids," is a favorite water sport in Finland. Large inflatable rafts, built to hold larger groups of people, are steered over the swift-flowing rapids that twist and turn near villages such as Käylä, in central Finland near the border with Russia. This is a popular sport for tourists, who can arrange organized trips based on the graded difficulty of the rivers. These operators also provide required safety equipment, including life jackets, waterproof clothing, rubber boots, and helmets, as well as the raft itself.

Perhaps surprisingly, harness racing is the second-most attended sport in Finland.

THE OLYMPICS

Finland first participated in the Olympics in 1908. Since then, the country has sent athletes to the largest organized sports event in the world every two years, for both the Summer and Winter Olympics. Finland holds the distinction, along with Sweden, of being one of only two nations to have earned medals at every Olympics since 1908. This is largely because of Finnish athletes' strength in winter sports such as cross-country skiing and ice hockey, as well as in summer sports like athletics, wrestling, shooting, and swimming.

The Finns are especially strong in the long-distance running and javelin events. Two runners in particular have made a name for themselves: Paavo Nurmi and Ville Ritola. Nurmi is the most famous Finnish athlete of all time. He won nine gold and three silver medals in the Olympics between 1920 and 1928. Ritola won five golds. In the 1970s the top name in running was Lasse

THE FINNISH SAUNA

If there is one single item that is quintessentially Finnish, it is the sauna. The sauna was traditionally used as a kind of bathhouse. When people lived in forests, they had a log cabin where they could keep a fire going to keep warm, relax, and wash themselves. Babies were also born in the sauna, as it was warm. And when houses had no shower or bathrooms, a weekly visit to the sauna was the only way to keep clean.

Today, the sauna has endured. Even though present-day homes are equipped with modern bathrooms, it is still a tradition for families and friends to get together in the sauna to relax. It has become a social ritual.

Many homes have private saunas, and there is a sauna in every apartment complex. Families with second homes by the lake and those living in rural areas have a separate log cabin housing the sauna, where they gather on Saturday evenings to relax. The sauna tradition is well suited to Finland's forests, which are the source of the sauna's building materials and fuel. The traditional smoke sauna, which has no chimney, is preferred, as the heat is said to be gentler. It takes seven hours to bring the sauna to the right temperature, and all smoke is expelled before anyone goes in. It is a tradition to jump into the lake to cool off between visits to the sauna or to roll in the snow during the winter months.

The Finns also use birch leaves to clean themselves in their sauna—it has the same effect as soap—and they hit each other with vihta *(VEE-ta) twigs to stimulate blood circulation and "beat out" tiredness from the body. After the cleansing ritual, the Finns*

indulge in a "sauna supper." Any Finn who invites a guest to take a sauna prepares a meal or at least coffee. While in the sauna, much salt is lost from the body due to perspiration, so salted dishes are usually served during the meal. These may include salted herring eaten with boiled potatoes, anchovies, smoked fish, sardines, or a salad of salted mushrooms.

Most Finnish urban homes even have their own saunas. These are small, high-tech, electric-operated saunas that heat up in a matter of minutes.

Virén, who won the 5,000-meter and 10,000-meter events in the 1972 and 1976 Olympics.

In javelin, Finland has scored sensational victories, particularly in the Olympics between 1908 and 1936. Even in modern times, Finnish javelin throwers continue to shine. In the 1988 Seoul Olympics, for instance, the Finns won the gold and bronze medals. In the 1992 Barcelona Olympics, the country walked away with a silver.

The Finns have also made a mark in other sports, such as canoeing. Top oarsman Perti Karpinnen, who was Finland's Sportsman of the Year in 1979 and 1980, and Mikko Kolehmainen, who won a gold in the 1992 Barcelona Games for canoeing, have boosted the popularity of the sport.

The Finns are also top contenders in winter sports, winning numerous gold medals in cross-country skiing in the Olympic winter games and world championships. Ski champions in the past included Veli Saarinen, Veikko Hakulinen, and Eero Mäntyranta among the men, and Helena Takalo and Hikka Riihivuori for the women.

Marja-Liisa Kirvesniemi was the darling of the nation when she won three gold medals and one bronze for cross-country skiing in the 1984 Sarajevo Winter Olympics. Her husband, Harri Kirvesniemi, is also a champion skier in his own right, having won medals in the Olympics and world championships. The latest skiing star is Marjo Matikainen, who won a gold and two bronze medals in the 1988 Calgary Winter Olympics.

The Finns are equally strong in ski jumping. The most famous Finnish ski jumper is world master and Olympic champion Matti Nykänen, who was unsurpassed in this event in the 1980s. In the Calgary Winter Olympics, he became the first ski jumper ever to win three golds in the same games. A ski jump is named after him in his hometown of Jyväskylä.

Toni Nieminen made a name for himself when he became the youngest winner ever in the history of the Winter Olympics. At seventeen years of age, he won two gold medals and one bronze for skiing in the 1992 Olympics in

Markku Uusipaavalniemi celebrates an Olympic win in curling in 2006.

Helsinki hosted the Summer Olympics in 1952.

Albertville, France. Nieminen also won a gold medal in the 1992 ski jumping World Cup.

Ice hockey is just as popular, with junior leagues formed for promising youngsters. Finnish players, like Jarri Kurri, have done so well that they have moved to the United States to join professional teams.

One of the country's top winter sportsmen is Janne Lahtela, who grabbed the gold in the men's moguls freestyle skiing event in the 2002 Winter Olympics held in Salt Lake City, Utah. Before that, he won a silver for the men's freestyle skiing event at Nagano in 1998. In the 2002 Olympics, Finland also won a team gold medal for the Nordic combined event, which involves competing in cross-country skiing and ski jumping.

In the 2006 Winter Olympics in Turin, a silver medal went to Tanja Pontiainen for the women's alpine skiing event while her compatriot, twenty-five-year-old Matti Hautamäki, fondly called "the Flying Young Finn," won a silver medal for ski jumping. He won a bronze for the same event in the 2002 Winter Olympics.

Markku Uusipaavalniemi, the country's top curler, brought home the silver medal for men's curling, a sport involving two teams sliding stones into a target circle, at the 2006 Olympics. Before that, in 2000, he led Finland's national curling team to victory at the European Curling Championship.

In the 2012 London Olympics, Finland took home a total of three metals. In the 2014 Sochi Olympics, Finnish athletes brought home a total of five metals, including a gold medal and two silvers in cross-country skiing, silver medals in snowboarding, and a bronze medal won by Finland's men's national hockey team.

MOTOR RACING

Motor sports have been a beloved national pastime since the 1950s and became cemented in the 1960s. Famous Finnish drivers include Rauno Aaltonen, Timo Mäkinen, and Pauli Toivonen. Juha Kankkunen and Tommi Mäkinen are legends in the field, and both won the World Rally Championship four times during their careers.

Pekka Vehkonen's reputation dominates motorcross racing, while Keke Rosberg achieved renown when he became Finland's first Formula One driver and the first Finn to win the world championship in 1982.

The most famous name in recent times is Mika Häkkinen, nicknamed "the Flying Finn." He was a member of the famous McLaren team, which is rated among the top teams in Formula One racing. Häkkinen competed for eleven seasons in the world's top motor racing event, the Formula One, winning twenty races and two world championships in 1998 and 1999. For years, he was the only real competition for German-born Michael Schumacher, holder of seven World Drivers' Championships since 1994. Häkkinen retired in 2001, handing over the wheel to his compatriot Kimi Räikkönen, another McLaren team member.

INTERNET LINKS

finland.fi/life-society/bare-facts-of-the-sauna
Finland's official website offers more information about the importance of the sauna in Finnish culture.

www.nationalparks.fi/hikinginfinland/rightsandregulations
Finland's National Parks website offers information about the famous everyman's rights in the country

FESTIVALS

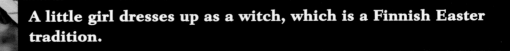

A little girl dresses up as a witch, which is a Finnish Easter tradition.

12

FINLAND OFFERS A LARGE RANGE OF festivals to appeal to any taste, from religious festivals dating back to pagan times to student festivals and large open-air music gatherings. Many of the festivals that are so dear to Finnish culture have been held, to some extent, since ancient times. These festivals are often linked with the changing of the seasons and harken back to a time when Finns worshipped many gods and spirits of nature in the hopes of controlling both the destruction and bounty of the natural world.

When Christianity was introduced to Finland in 1000 CE, it could not erase the gods and religious traditions that had been engrained in Finnish culture for thousands of years. Instead, Finns incorporated their new Christian beliefs into these ancient rituals. This rich intermingling of native Finnish belief and Christian imported beliefs still exists in the modern traditions and festivals celebrated today.

Folk traditions and customs from Sweden, Russia, and Germany exist alongside Christian beliefs to create the many Finnish holidays and celebrations observed in a year.

EASTER TRADITIONS

Finns celebrate the Christian holiday of Easter in a way that honors their ancient traditions, too. In Finnish tradition, young children—especially girls—dress up as Easter witches and go door-to-door with branches decorated with colorful feathers and crepe paper, seeking treats in return for chasing away evil spirits. Homeowners usually keep a basket of chocolate eggs by the door to reward these little Easter witches. This custom is derived from ancient Pagan traditions and Russian Orthodox rituals where twigs represented the palm fronds that welcomed Jesus into Jerusalem on Palm Sunday. It is also linked to western Finnish traditions that parodied earlier fears of witches roaming about on Easter.

Bonfires also play an important role in traditional Easter rituals. Linked with early customs that prevented spirits from harming farm cattle in rural Finland, these contemporary bonfires drive away evil spirits on the Saturday night before Easter.

LENTEN HOLIDAYS

Shrove Tuesday takes place seven weeks before Easter, the day before Ash Wednesday. Known as Laskiainen (LAS-kee-eye-nen) in Finnish, the day is typically celebrated by serving green pea soup for the family meal, followed by a pastry filled with whipped cream and served with jam called *laskiaispulla*. Oftentimes, religious celebrations on Shrove Tuesday are followed by a trip down a snowy hill on a sled.

NATIONAL SLEEPY HEAD DAY

A fun and uniquely Finnish holiday, National Sleepy Head Day is celebrated each year on July 27. The holiday traces its origins back to a religious story about seven youths, known as "the seven sleepers," who hid in a cave near Ephesus, Turkey, to escape persecution for their belief in god in the early third century. Far from a high religious holiday, however, National Sleepy Head Day—called Unikeonpäivä (OO-nee-KAY-on-pai-va) in Finnish—has become a fun informal celebration. According to custom, anyone who sleeps late on this day will be lazy for the rest of the year. Each year, in the city of Naantali, a celebrity "sleeper" is chosen to be thrown into the sea. Townspeople flock to see who the chosen celebrity will be, as it is kept secret until the event itself.

CHRISTMAS

Christmas is the most important Christian holiday in Finland. Finns celebrate the

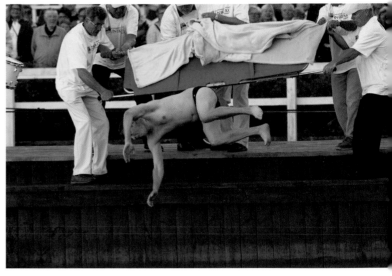

A "sleeper" is thrown into the water during traditional Sleepy Head celebrations in Naantali.

religious holiday through the popular figure of Santa Claus, who, according to Finnish tradition, lives in Lapland. Christmas, known in Finnish as Joulu (YO-lo), coincides with the winter solstice, the darkest day of the year. This day also signaled the end of the harvest during ancient times. For ancient peoples, the winter solstice, which later became integrated into the Christian holiday of Christmas, was a time for celebration in the face of the dark and cold days that awaited them.

The Christmas tree was only introduced in the last century but has become an integral part of the Finnish holiday season. Originally, Father Christmas appeared in the form of a goat and threw presents into the doorways of houses. The appearance of a goat stemmed from pagan days when the worship of Thor, the Swedish god of thunder, included the worship of his goat. In the past, someone carrying a goat's head would burst into the parties of merrymakers. After nightlong celebrations of singing and dancing, the goat would "die" and then return to life.

In 1927, a children's radio program introduced the modern Father Christmas who brought gifts to children from his home in Lapland in his reindeer-drawn sleigh. The notion stuck. Today, children the world over are enticed to spend winter holidays in Lapland with Santa Claus. His "home" is decked with all kinds of Christmas-related items, and he answers letters sent by those unable to visit him in person.

SAINT STEPHEN'S DAY

On the heels of Christmas comes Saint Stephen's Day, known as Tapaninpäivä (TAH-pa-neen-PAI-va), a holiday that commemorates the first Christian martyr. Celebrated on December 26, Finns typically ride in sleighs drawn by horses to honor Saint Stephen, who is the patron saint of horses. The jingle of bells can be heard in the streets of many Finnish towns and villages on this day, and sometimes parades are held with singers who cover festive holiday tunes. In many other countries, this day is known as Boxing Day.

MIDSUMMER EVE

Midsummer Eve is an important holiday in Finland, where celebrations began in ancient times to commemorate the longest day of the year. In many areas of Finland, the sun does not set on this day and partygoers enjoy the midnight sun—and the parties that go along with it—until the wee hours of the morning, when they will eventually head to bed.

Known as Juhannus (YOO-hahn-oos) in Finland, after Saint John the Baptist, the celebration is said to be Christian in origin. It was believed that the doors of the underworld were open on this day, letting out spirits and ghosts to roam the streets and infest the air. Thousands of bonfires are lit in the belief that, by burning a bonfire, the air will be purified so that the spirits can do no harm.

Others believe that the event is more likely a folk tradition associated with this magical, nightless day. That it is the day of the most light is reason enough for merrymaking. It was also a celebration associated with growth, life, and fertility.

Cattle were decorated with garlands of flowers, while young maidens would sleep with a sprig of nine herbs under their pillows so that they would dream of their future bridegrooms. If girls looked into a pool of water, it was said that they could see the face of their sweetheart. Many of these customs are still practiced today as a source of amusement.

Other customs date back to pre-Christian times, when magic was used to promote a bountiful harvest and fertility in the coming year. Houses, boats, and buses are covered with fresh birch branches. In many places in Finland, doorways continue to be adorned with young birch trees, while those living on the Swedish-speaking Åland Islands put up midsummer poles. These poles, erected in the midst of a bonfire pile, are decorated with wooden ships and boats, and people dance around them. Midsummer supper tables are decorated with birch and flowers.

Midsummer bonfires are lit throughout Finland. Families and friends gather at lakeside cottages to make their own bonfires, dancing around them and singing traditional songs. They stay up all night celebrating. The biggest bonfire in Helsinki is at the Seurasaari open-air folk museum, where cultural dances are also held as part of the festivities.

NAME DAYS

In Finland, everyone has two "birthdays" a year: one on the day of their birth, and one on their name day. Each day on the Finnish calendar coincides with a name, typically the name of a saint. If your name matches with the name on the calendar that day, then it is your day to celebrate. This celebration is Roman Catholic in origin, as a way of honoring Catholic saints.

It is customary for friends and relatives to wish one a "Happy name day" and to give the person flowers and presents on his or her name day. The occasion is also celebrated with a birthday cake and candles.

Ruut (Ruth) Rotko, who celebrates her name day on January 4 and her birthday on May 27, says, "People always know your Name Day but not necessarily your birthday."

NATIONAL INDEPENDENCE DAY

December 6 marks Finland's Independence Day, an important holiday that commemorates the country's official separation from Russia in 1917. In the early years, Independence Day was a somber occasion, usually marked with political speeches and visits to church. Today, however, the holiday has become much more festive.

Helsinki is the most important place for celebrations, which start at 9:00 a.m. with a flag-raising ceremony. A commemorative daytime service is then held. In the afternoon, there is a procession from the Hietaniemi Graveyard to Senate Square. This solemn procession of university students is perhaps the most moving of all the commemorative ceremonies. The event is held to remember those who died helping Finland gain its independence. Lighted candles are placed on the graves to burn all evening, illuminating the dark, snowy stillness—a befitting end to the day's events.

MAY DAY AND STUDENTS' DAY

Like other Finnish celebrations, May Day, on May 1, originated as a pagan holiday to celebrate the coming of spring. Today, worldwide celebrations of May Day typically focus on honoring laborers and labor activism. Finland's festivities combine this with a traditional festival honoring university students toward the end of the school year. Typically, May Day is celebrated with noisy parades, concerts, fairs, and speeches. Colorful balloons and flowers line the streets of Finnish cities. There are lots of boisterous partygoers in the street, anxious to celebrate the coming of spring.

For the Students' Day celebrations on May Day, university students wear a white cap, a symbol of their high school graduation. At 6:00 p.m. on May Day Eve, students in Helsinki gather around the statue of a mermaid near the harbor. Known as the Havis Amanda, this statue depicts the symbol of Finland. Students cap the mermaid statue with their hats while crowds gather around to watch. On the next day, May 1, students gather around parks and campuses to listen to student speakers and picnic.

FINNISH NEW YEAR'S EVE TRADITIONS

Besides May Day, New Year's Eve is the most boisterous event on the Finnish calendar. Finnish stores sell small firecrackers that can only be used on New Year's Eve between 6:00 p.m. and 2:00 a.m. the next morning. When the clock strikes midnight, the Finns yell, "Hyvää uutta vuotta!," which means "Happy New Year," and kiss each other on the cheeks.

CALENDAR OF PUBLIC HOLIDAYS

New Year's Day . . . . January 1

Epiphany . . . . January 6

Good Friday . . . . March/April

Easter . . . . March/April

May Day . . . . May 1

Ascension Day . . . . May

Whitsun . . . . May

Midsummer's Day . . . . third weekend in June

All Saints' Day . . . . November 1

Independence Day . . . . December 6

Christmas Day . . . . December 25

Boxing Day/Saint Stephen's Day . . . . . December 26

A Finnish New Year's tradition is to melt a small amount of tin in a pan before throwing it into a bucket of water where it is left to harden. The form of the solidified tin is supposed to offer a glimpse into what the new year holds. Lumps signify an increase in wealth, black spots warn of impending sadness, and boat-like shapes predict upcoming travel.

INTERNET LINKS

en.biginfinland.com/unikeonpaiva-sleepys-head-day-finland
This Finnish site offers information about this fun holiday.

www.frommers.com/destinations/finland/760260
This Frommer's website lists several of Finland's most famous festivals and celebrations.

FOOD

Fresh, seasonal produce is the highlight of Finnish cuisine. Here, Finnish cheese is paired with cloudberries for a sweet treat.

13

TRADITIONAL FINNISH CUISINE

is a unique blend of Russian and Swedish influences, combined with other culinary traditions, which produces hearty, vegetable- and meat-laden meals. In addition to foreign cultural influences, Finland's cuisine is known for blending the rustic culinary traditions of its countryside with so-called haute, or high contemporary, cuisine. Specialties depend on the region and the season, with meals depending on the seasonal bounty provided by Finland's lush lands.

Many of Finland's most well-known recipes have been passed down from one generation to another, over hundreds of years. These recipes can be simple and depend on the freshest ingredients. Traditionally, Finland's long winters mean that fresh vegetables and fruit are not always available. Thus, many traditional recipes depend on tubers, like potatoes and turnips, as staples. Rye bread is almost always served on the side of any meal.

In the north, recipes often make use of reindeer meat, but pork and beef are also widely used. Given the Finns' proclivity to hunting, wild meats, including deer and moose, are also regularly served, as well as smaller game animals, such as rabbit and duck. Fish also plays a

While the Finns value their foods fresh and seasonal, they also like the occasional quick, and not so healthy, meal. Fast-food chain restaurant Hesburger is the Finnish equivalent of McDonald's and many Finns state that their Hesburger fries taste better than McDonald's fries!

prominent role in Finnish cuisine. The thousands of lakes spread across the country provide ample opportunity for fresh fish, including salmon, Baltic herring, and whitefish. Crayfish is popular when it is seasonally available, from July through September, and many Finnish summer parties prominently display this delicacy.

Oftentimes, fish is cold smoked or pickled and eaten on toast or with an accompaniment of small potatoes. Due to Swedish influence in particular, smoked herring and pickled herring are popular choices. Some fish can be served raw, too, especially fresh salmon, which is served with lemon juice.

Wild berries, which grow abundantly even in Finland's Arctic region, are another prominent feature of Finnish cuisine. While berries are eaten fresh in the summer, they are often dried and enjoyed throughout the year. Some berries native to Finland are familiar to foreigners, such as raspberries, cranberries, and strawberries, while other berries are particularly Scandinavian in culture, like lingonberries and bilberries. Cloudberries are particularly viewed as a delicacy, with their creamy texture and tart taste, and they are often made into jams and juices. Cloudberries are often eaten with warmed cheese called *leipäjuusto* and topped with cream or sugar.

It is common for families to spend lazy summer days hunting for wild berries. In the fall, many families turn their hunts to foraging for wild mushrooms, including chanterelles and morels. These mushrooms can be made into a delicious soup known as *korvasienikeitto* (KORR-va-sie-ni-KAY-ee-toh). Many of the other recipes that revolve around mushrooms in Finland, including sauces and stews, can be traced back to Russian cuisine. Those mushrooms that are not immediately used can be preserved for the winter by drying or pickling them.

In the winter, the day may start with a warm bowl of porridge using rolled oats or rye. For the Christmas season, milk-based porridge is enjoyed with cinnamon, sugar, and thickened prune juice. Body-warming soups and pies are also popular, including fish-based soups such as *lohikeitto* (LOH-i-KAY-ee-toh), which is salmon soup with potatoes, dill, and milk. In February *mäti* (MA-tee), a roe from freshwater fish, is served as a specialty. Referred to as Finnish caviar, this roe is yellow or orange in color and can be served with buckwheat blinis, chopped onions, or just thick sour cream.

SWEDISH INFLUENCE

Smorgasbord is one of the most visible influences of Swedish cuisine in Finland. Although it is Swedish in origin, the Finns have made smorgasbord their own. Foreigners staying in hotels will often be served a smorgasbord for breakfast or lunch, consisting of a wide range of dishes, often including smoked salmon, salami, cheeses, and salads. Smorgasbord offers a great opportunity to try a variety of Finnish dishes.

While Swedish cuisine has greatly influenced Finnish meals, there remains one big difference between the countries' dishes. Swedish food tends to be sweeter than Finnish dishes, with Finns tending to prefer unsweetened food.

Finnish smorgasbord was adopted from traditionally Swedish cuisine.

HOLIDAY FARE

As in other countries, Christmas is a time for feasting. In the traditional rice porridge eaten for breakfast during the Christmas season, family members hide an almond. Whoever finds the almond in their dish must "pay" a penalty, which can be singing a song or reciting a poem. Oftentimes, the days before Christmas are filled not only with Christmas shopping, but selecting the freshest ingredients for the *joulupöytä*, or the "Christmas table," in which many traditional Christmas recipes are offered to guests and families throughout the holidays.

In the early evening, many people go to the cemetery to spare a moment of thought for their departed ones. They pray and light candles on family graves. Then, it is time to enjoy a sauna before sitting down to feast.

A glass of warming grogg or spiced mulled wine is first served as an aperitif to get the party going. The meal itself begins with lightly salted salmon, herring prepared in various ways, and other types of cold hors d'oeuvres. The

Karelian vegetable pastries are a regional treat.

main dish is glazed ham cooked overnight in a slow oven. It is accompanied by other oven-baked dishes made from carrots, potatoes, rutabagas, and liver, and slices of a sweet and spicy Christmas bread. A home-brewed ale is traditionally drunk at Christmas. Dessert may be prune parfait or pies made from berries. The rest of the evening is spent at home, chatting and drinking in front of a fire.

Christmas Day starts early, when Finnish families go to church. Then, it is time for more feasting on rich Christmas pies such as *joulutorttu* (YO-loo-TORR-too) or tiny delectable pastries stuffed with pulped prunes, gingerbread, dates, and fruitcake. Boxing Day on December 26 is reserved for visiting friends and relatives and finishing the Christmas leftovers. A dance in the evening usually marks the end of the festive season.

REGIONAL DISHES

While Finland has many regional treats, certain areas of the country are better known for their cuisine than others. In particular, Karelia in the east of the country is known for its meat pastries and casseroles. *Karjalanpaisti* (KAR-yah-lahn-PA-I-stee) is a Karelian meat casserole, a hearty blend of beef, pork, and mutton, eaten traditionally in winter. *Karjalanpiirakat* (KAR-yah-lahn-PEE-rah-kaht) are Karelian pastries made of rye dough that are filled with rice or mashed potatoes and served hot alongside hard-boiled eggs and butter. Also from eastern Finland, particularly Kuopio, is *kalakukko* (KAH-lah-KOO-ko), which is fish and bacon baked inside a crust of rye bread.

Eating reindeer is typically Finnish, and reindeer meat can be prepared in various ways and eaten in many forms, grilled as steaks or chops, or cooked in stews. In Lapland, *poronpaisti* (POH-ron-PA-I-stee), a reindeer roast, and *poronkäristys* (POh-rohn-KA-rees-toos), which are thin strips of smoked reindeer meat, are common. *Mustamakkara* (MUST-ah-MAH-ka-ra) is grilled black pudding, a Tampere specialty, served with red whortleberries.

FINNISH SPIRITS

The Finns are known for making a wide variety of drinks, out of fresh ingredients. In particular, the country is known for its berry liquors and its grain spirits. *Lakkalikööri* (LAK-ka-LEE-koo-ee-ree) is made from golden-yellow cloudberries that grow on arctic and subarctic bogs. The rich, strong-flavored liqueur is reputedly full of vitamin C. Another strong berry liqueur is *puolukkalikööri* (POO-loo-kah-LEE-koo-ee-ree), made from red whortleberries or cowberries. The rare arctic brambleberry, which looks like a wild strawberry, makes a sweet but delicate liqueur called *mesimarjalikööri* (MES-see-mar-ya-LEE-koo-ee-ree). The best-known Finnish grain spirit is Finlandia vodka, which comes in a frosted bottle. The Finns have their own version of champagne—a sparkling wine fermented from white currants and gooseberries.

INTERNET LINKS

www.food.com/topic/finnish
This site compiles all of Food.com's Finnish recipes.

www.visitfinland.com/article/iconic-finnish-foods-of-all-time
Find information and beautiful pictures of the most iconic Finnish foods here.

FINNISH PULLA

½ cup warm water
¼ ounce active dry yeast
1 cup white sugar
1 teaspoon salt
1 teaspoon ground cardamom
4 eggs, beaten
9 cups flour
½ cup melted butter

Heat the milk in a saucepan until it bubbles, then quickly remove it from the heat and let it cool slightly. Dissolve yeast in the warm water, then mix in lukewarm milk, sugar, salt, cardamom, eggs, and flour. Add the melted butter and stir well. Let the dough rest on the counter under an inverted bowl for fifteen minutes. Then knead it and put it into a greased bowl, cover with a clean towel, and let it rise for approximately one hour. After it has doubled in size, divide it into equal strips. Braid the strips together to form a large loaf and allow it to rise again for twenty minutes. Brush with egg wash and sprinkle with sugar before placing it in a 400°F (205°C) oven for twenty-five to thirty minutes.

FINNISH SUMMER SOUP

2 cups water

5 small potatoes, peeled and halved

12 baby carrots

2 tablespoons butter

1 ½ pounds fresh green beans

2 cups peas

2 cups half-and-half

3 tablespoons flour

2 tablespoons butter

⅛ teaspoon ground black pepper

1 teaspoon salt

Boil the potatoes in the water until tender, approximately twenty minutes. Add butter, onions, carrots, green beans, butter, salt, and pepper. When vegetables are tender, add the peas.

In a small bowl, stir together half-and-half and flour until combined. Then add this mixture to the vegetables. Cook until the soup is slightly thickened and serve.

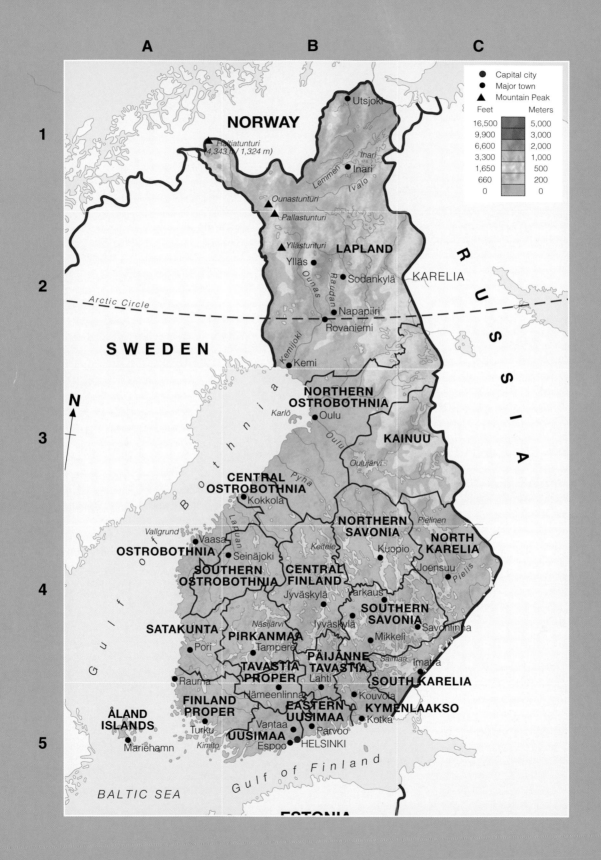

MAP OF FINLAND

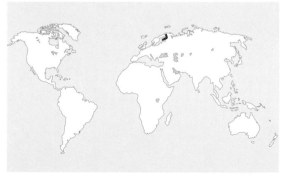

ECONOMIC FINLAND

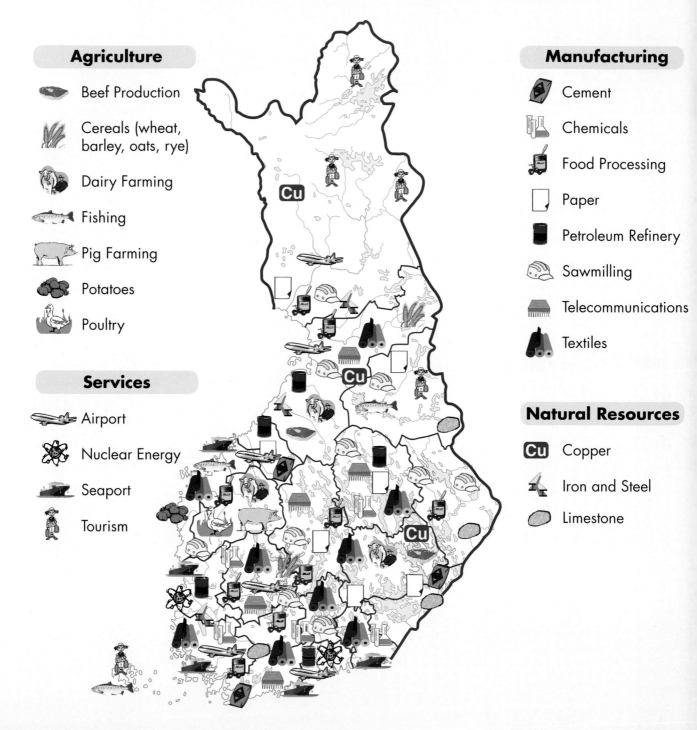

Agriculture

- Beef Production
- Cereals (wheat, barley, oats, rye)
- Dairy Farming
- Fishing
- Pig Farming
- Potatoes
- Poultry

Services

- Airport
- Nuclear Energy
- Seaport
- Tourism

Manufacturing

- Cement
- Chemicals
- Food Processing
- Paper
- Petroleum Refinery
- Sawmilling
- Telecommunications
- Textiles

Natural Resources

- Cu Copper
- Iron and Steel
- Limestone

ABOUT THE ECONOMY

OVERVIEW

Finland began its transition from a largely rural society to a modern, industrialized nation after the end of World War II. In 1991, Finland experienced its first recession, during which the economy took a nosedive and unemployment skyrocketed. Finland was last affected by the global economic crisis in 2008. Its gross domestic product shrank slightly in 2015, although its overall growth level has strengthened since 2011.

GROSS DOMESTIC PRODUCT (GDP)

$229.8 billion (2015)

GDP GROWTH

0.6 percent (2016)

LAND USE

Arable land 8 percent, forest 78 percent, other 14 percent

CURRENCY

The euro (EUR), converted from the former markka in 2002; 1 euro = 5.95 markkas; the euro is divided into 100 cents; USD1 = .90 euro (August 2016)

MINERAL RESOURCES

Iron ore, copper, lead, zinc, chromite, nickel, gold, silver, limestone

AGRICULTURAL PRODUCTS

Grain (wheat, barley, oats, rye), beetroot, spinach, rutabaga, potato, cabbage, forest products, dairy farming, beef, pigs, poultry

MAJOR EXPORTS

Electronic and electrical products, refined petroleum, pulp and paper, machinery and equipment, metal products, transportation vehicles, timber and wood, chemicals

EXPORTS OF GOODS AND SERVICES

$85.64 billion (2015)

MAJOR IMPORTS

Petroleum and petroleum products, chemicals, transportation equipment, iron and steel, machinery, foodstuffs, grain, textile yarn and fabrics

IMPORTS OF GOODS AND SERVICES

$76.88 billion (2015)

TRADE PARTNERS

Germany, Netherlands, Russia, Sweden, United Kingdom, United States

WORKFORCE

2.7 million (2015)

UNEMPLOYMENT RATE

9.4 percent (2015)

INFLATION RATE

1.21 percent (2015)

CULTURAL FINLAND

Ylläs

Ylläs is one of Finland's top ski centers and host to a music festival in July.

Rovaniemi

Gateway to Lapland, home of the Sami people, and the start of the Great Arctic Highway, Rovaniemi is the place to see the famous Aurora Borealis, or nothern lights, a mysterious glow that lights up the sky on winter nights.

Kemi

It is here that one can cruise the Gulf of Bothnia on board an Arctic icebreaker for a quintessentially Finnish experience.

Pori

A music lover's haven in mid-July, when the ten-day Pori International Jazz Festival takes place, Pori offers a smorgasbord of more than one hundred performances by the world's best jazz musicians.

Rauma

A UNESCO World Heritage site, Rauma's Old Town is a pedestrian's delight with its six hundred wooden buildings from the eighteenth and nineteenth centuries.

Turku

Founded in the thirteenth century, Turku was Finland's capital until 1812 and is the seat of the country's first university. Turku is billed as the country's cultural capital, and one of its top attractions is its outstanding medieval Turku Castle.

Åland

A slice of Sweden in Finland, visitors can go cruising in a wooden schooner among its 6,400 islets, enjoy traditional midsummer festivities with maypole dancing, or visit its fourteenth-century Kastelholm Castle.

Inari

The hub of Sami culture. Visitors can learn more about Sami culture at the open-air Siida Sami Museum, which showcases Sami history and lifestyle, and visit a reindeer farm or explore the wilderness here.

Napapiiri

This is where the Arctic Circle officially begins. It is the site of the well-known Santa Claus Village, the "official" home of Santa Claus, who may be visited in his Santapark office.

Oulanka National Park
For true wilderness experience and some of the best scenery in all of Finland, visitors may roam the fells here and stay in a wilderness hut.

Oulu
Visitors travel from different parts of the world to experience the land of the midnight sun in June and July when the sun never sets, and revel in this lively university town's outdoor bars and summer festivals.

Savonlinna
Set on two islands between two lakes, Savonlinna provides a beautiful setting for the renowned month-long Savonlinna Opera Festival in July, attracting top opera performers. The festival is held in the courtyard of Olavinlinna, the best preserved medieval castle in Scandinavia.

Ilomantsi
Ilomantsi is Karelia at its best. It is more Russian than Finish in culture and is the seat of the Orthodox Church.

Lappeenranta

Set on the shores of Lake Saimaa and only 18.6 miles (30 km) from the Russian border, it is the biggest inland port in Finland. Visitors may embark on the MS *Karelia* for a day-long cruise on the historic canal to Vyborg in Russia.

Helsinki
The capital of Finland since 1812, this beautiful maritime city is more cosmopolitan than truly Scandinavian, thanks to its mix of Swedish, Russian, and international influences. A cultural and high-tech hub, it is noted for active concert scene and nightlife.

ABOUT THE CULTURE

OFFICIAL NAME
Republic of Finland
In Finnish—Suomen Tasavalta (Suomi, in abbreviated form)
In Swedish—Republiken Finland (Finland, in abbreviated form)

FLAG DESCRIPTION
The national (civil) flag of Finland is a blue rectangular Scandinavian cross on a white background. The state flag, used by the military, bears the state arms on the intersection of the cross.

TOTAL AREA
130,558 square miles (338,144 sq km)

CAPITAL
Helsinki

POPULATION
5.44 million (2013)

ETHNIC GROUPS
Finn 93.4 percent, Swede 5.6 percent, Russian 0.5 percent, Estonian 0.3 percent, Roma 0.1 percent, Sami 0.1 percent

RELIGIOUS GROUPS
Lutheran National Church 77 percent, Orthodox Church 1 percent, other Christian denominations 1.1 percent, others 0.1 percent, .8 percent Muslim, non-affiliated 19 percent

BIRTH RATE
10.7 births per 1,000 Finns (2013 estimate)

DEATH RATE
9.5 deaths per 1,000 Finns (2013 estimate)

AGE STRUCTURE
0 to 14 years: 15.8 percent (male 423,011/female 408,664);
15 to 64 years: 64.4 percent (male 1,716,293 female 1,677,001);
65 years and over: 19.8 percent (male 439,014/female 604,816) (2015 estimates)

LANGUAGES
Finnish (official), Swedish (official), Sami (official minority), Romani (official minority), Finnish Sign Language (official minority), Karelian (official minority)

LITERACY RATE
For those aged 15 and above who can both read and write: 100 percent

NATIONAL HOLIDAYS
New Year's Day (January 1), Twelfth Day (January 6), Good Friday, Easter Sunday, May Day (May 1), Ascension Day, Midsummer Day (June 24), All Saints' Day (November 1), Independence Day (December 12), Christmas Day (December 25), Boxing Day (December 26)

TIMELINE

IN FINLAND	IN THE WORLD

7,500–1,500 BCE (Stone Age)
Tribes believed to be the ancestors of the Sami arrive from eastern Europe and settle on the Arctic coast of present-day Finland. Later settlers caused the Sami to move farther north.

753 BCE
Rome is founded.

500 BCE– 400 CE
The Finns, who gave the country its name, cross the Baltic to settle in Finland.

116–17 BCE
The Roman Empire reaches its greatest extent, under Emperor Trajan (98–17).

600 CE
Height of the Mayan civilization.

1000
The Chinese perfect gunpowder and begin to use it in warfare.

1528
The Reformation reaches Finland with Mikael Agricola introducing the teachings of Martin Luther. Finland breaks away from the Catholic Church.

1530
Beginning of transatlantic slave trade organized by the Portuguese in Africa.

1550
Founding of Helsinki, or Helsingfors, by the Swedish king.

1558–1603
Reign of Elizabeth I of England.

1620
Pilgrims sail the *Mayflower* to America.

1714–1721
The Great Wrath, the occupation of Finland by Russia, ends in 1721, with the Treaty of Uusikaupunki.

1776
US Declaration of Independence.

1741–1743
The War of the Hats begins with Sweden attacking eastern Karelia, which is under Russian control. Russia counterattacks and occupies all of Finland in 1742, a period known as the Lesser Wrath. It ends in 1743 with the Treaty of Turku.

1789–1799
The French Revolution.

1809
Finland becomes an autonomous Grand Duchy of Russia. The Finns retain their own legal system and religion and are exempt from Russian military service.

1812
The Russians move the capital of Finland from Turku to Helsinki.

1861
The US Civil War begins.

1906
Finnish women are given the right to vote—the first in Europe.

1869
The Suez Canal is opened.

IN FINLAND	IN THE WORLD
	1914 World War I begins.
1917 The Russian Revolution begins, and Finland declares its independence.	
1939 World War II begins. Finland declares its neutrality but is invaded by the Soviet Union. Winter War between the two countries starts.	**1939** World War II begins. **1945** The United States drops atomic bombs on Hiroshima and Nagasaki. **1949** The North Atlantic Treaty Organization (NATO) is formed.
1995 Finland becomes a member of the European Union (EU), formerly known as the European Economic Community.	**1991** Breakup of the Soviet Union.
1999 Finland serves as president of the EU and hosts two head of state summits.	**1997** Hong Kong is returned to China.
2000 Finland elects its first female president, Tarja Halonen, in February. On March 1, Finland's new constitution comes into force.	**2001** Terrorists crash planes in New York, Washington, DC, and Pennsylvania.
2003 Finland elects its first female prime minister, Anneli Jäätteenmäki. Matti Vanhanen takes over as premier.	**2003** War in Iraq begins.
2006 Tarja Halonen is reelected as president for a second term in January.	**2008** A global economic crisis begins in the United States and spreads worldwide.
2012 The first conservative president since 1956, Sauli Niinisto, wins the election.	
2016 Many asylum seekers in Finland move elsewhere due to Finland's frigid temperatures.	**2016** Terror attacks associated with the rise of the Islamic State (IS) kill many across France, Turkey, the United States, Afghanistan, and Pakistan, in addition to the civil conflicts in Iraq and Syria.

GLOSSARY

ei (ay)
No.

eskers
Long level ridges of sand and rock left behind when glaciers melt and recede.

Joulu (YO-lo)
The Christmas holiday.

Juhannus (YOO-hahn-oos)
Midsummer celebration held on June 23, usually highlighted by a bonfire.

kaamos (KAAH-mos)
"Sunless days" in the Arctic region when the sun never rises. This season lasts nearly six months.

kantele (KAHN-tay-leh)
An ancient harp-like instrument traditionally used to accompany rune singers.

kiitos (KEEH-tos)
Thank you.

korvasienikeitto (KORR-va-sie-ni-KAY-ee-toh)
A light, creamy soup.

kyllä (KOO-la)
Yes.

lohikeitto (LOH-i-KAY-ee-toh)
A salmon soup.

mäti (MA-tee)
Roe from a freshwater fish.

näkemiin (NA-kem-een)
Good-bye.

olkaa hyvä (OHL-kaah HOO-vah)
Please.

pesäpallo (PAY-sa-PAHL-lo)
A type of baseball game.

poronpaisti (POH-ron-PA-I-ees-tee)
A reindeer roast.

pulla (POO-lah)
Sweet bread flavored with cardamom and sprinkled with sugar.

saari (SAAH-ri)
Island.

Tapaninpäivä (TAH-pa-neen-PAI-va)
Boxing Day, on December 26.

FOR FURTHER INFORMATION

BOOKS

Hill, Anja. *Classic Recipes of Finland: Traditional food and Cooking in 25 Authentic Dishes.* London: Lorenz Books, 2015.

Jansson, Tove. *Tales from Moominvalley.* New York: Puffin Books, 2003.

Lönnrot, Elias. *The Kalevala: or Poems of the Kaleva District.* Translated by Francis Peabody Magoun, Jr. Cambridge, MA: Harvard University Press, 2006.

Moles, Tarja. *Xenophobe's Guide to the Finns.* London: Oval Books, 2011.

Partanen, Anu. *The Nordic Theory of Everything: In Search of a Better Life.* New York: Harper, 2016.

Singleton, Frederick B. *A Short History of Finland.* New York: Cambridge University Press, 1990.

WEBSITES

Embassy of Finland, Washington, DC. http://www.finland.org/en

The Official Travel Guide of Finland. http://www.visitfinland.com

Virtual Finland. http://virtual.finland.fi

MUSIC

Various Artists. *Finland: Traditional Music.* Ocora, 1996.

MOVIES

Helsinki, Forever. Directed by Peter Von Bagh, 2008.

Steam of Life. Directed by Joonas Berghäll and Mika Hotakainen, 2011.

BIBLIOGRAPHY

Association of Finnish Symphony Orchestras. http://www.sinfoniaorkesterit.fi/en.

Charbonneau, Claudette, and S. W. Meditz. *The Land and People of Finland*. New York: J. B. Lippincott, 1990.

City of Helsinki. "Events Calendars." http://www.hel.fi/www/Helsinki/en/culture/events/Event-calendars.

Dance Info Finland. http://www.danceinfo.fi/en.

Design Museum. http://www.designmuseum.fi/en.

Finland Festivals. http://www.festivals.fi/en.

Lerner Publications Company Geography Department and David A. Boehm, ed. *Finland—in Pictures*. Minneapolis, MN: Lerner Publications Company, 1991.

Ministry of Education and Culture. http://www.minedu.fi/OPM/?lang=en.

Museums. http://www.museot.fi/en.php.

Music Finland. http://www.musicfinland.fi/en.

Rajanen, Ani. *Of Finnish Ways*. New York: HarperCollins, 1990.

Singleton, Frederick B. *A Short History of Finland*. New York: Cambridge University Press, 1990.

Solsten, Eric, and Meditz, S. W. eds. *Finland: A Country Study*. 2nd edition. Washington DC: US Government Printing Office, 1991.

This Is Finland. http://www.finland.fi.

Vaananen-Jensen, Inkeri, trans. *The Fish of Gold and Other Finnish Folk Tales*. Iowa City, IA: Penfield Press, 1990.

INDEX

INDEX